THE SPIRIT OF THE LORD IS UPON ME

The Writings of Suzanne Hiatt

THE SPIRIT OF THE LORD IS UPON ME

The Writings of Suzanne Hiatt

CARTER HEYWARD

and

JANINE LEHANE

Editors

 Seabury Books
NEW YORK

Unless otherwise noted, the Scripture quotations contained herein are from the New Revised Standard Version Bible, copyright © 1989 by the Division of Christian Education of the National Council of Churches of Christ in the U.S.A. Used by permission. All rights reserved.

Library of Congress Cataloging-in-Publication Data

Hiatt, Suzanne R.
  [Sermons. Selections]
  The spirit of the Lord is upon me : the writings of Suzanne Hiatt / Carter Heyward and Janine Lehane, editors.
    pages   cm
  Includes bibliographical references.
  ISBN 978-1-59627-262-0 (pbk.) -- ISBN 978-1-59627-263-7 (ebook) 1. Ordi-nation of women--Episcopal Church--Sermons. 2. Episcopal Church—Sermons. I. Heyward, Carter, editor of compilation. II. Title.
  BV676.H53   2014
  262'.14373082—dc23
                                                          2013049214

Seabury Books
19 East 34th Street
New York, New York 10016
www.churchpublishing.org
An imprint of Church Publishing Incorporated

Cover design by Laurie Klein Westhafer
Interior design and typesetting by Beth Oberholtzer

Printed in the United States of America

Soulboat

For Suzanne Radley Hiatt
High Spring, 2001

May you be launched
in fair weather,
with the wind
at your back
and the shining stars
streaming you through
the whole map of heaven.

May your strong sails
of bright silk billow,
proud and free
with the sun's golden blessing,
and carry you, safe and well
and all the way home.

▮▮▮

Tell your children lest they forget
and fall into danger—remind them
even they were not born in freedom,
but under a bondage they no longer
remember, which is still with them,
if unseen.

Bozarth, Alla Renée, excerpt from "Passover Remembered," *Womanpriest: A Personal Odyssey*, revised edition, Luramedia 1988, distributed by Wisdom House, 43222 SE Tapp Rd., Sandy, Oregon 97055; and *Stars in Your Bones: Emerging Signposts on Our Spiritual Journeys*, Alla Bozarth, Julia Barkley and Terri Hawthorne, North Star Press of St. Cloud 1990. All rights reserved. For permission to reprint, write to the poet at: allabearheart@yahoo.com.

❋ ❋ ❋

The Rev. Suzanne Radley Hiatt

Sept. 21, 1936	Born in Hartford, Connecticut.
1942	Family moved to Minneapolis, Minnesota, where Sue attended grammar school and high school.
June 1958	BA cum laude, Radcliffe College, Cambridge, Massachusetts. Major: American History.
1958–60	District Director, Greater Hartford Girl Scouts, Hartford, Connecticut. Organizational work with suburban adult volunteers, direct work with ghetto youngsters. Public relations and camp administration.
1961	Teacher, Weaver High School, Hartford, Connecticut. Taught high school English in the ghetto.
June 1964	MDiv cum laude, Episcopal Theological School, Cambridge, Massachusetts.
June 1965	MSW, Boston University School of Social Work, Boston, Massachusetts. Major: Casework.
1966–67	Parish Assistant, Dayton Avenue Presbyterian Church, St. Paul, Minnesota. Part of ecumenical team ministry in ghetto church. Casework with families, administered OEO tutoring project, community organization in American Indian community.

1967–68	Assistant consultant in public welfare for the Health and Welfare Council of Philadelphia. Helped organize Philadelphia Welfare Rights Organization.
1968–1972	Suburban Missioner, Episcopal Diocese of Pennsylvania. Worked with suburban church members to create roles for participating in the solution of urban problems. Community organization in suburban communities. Member, Academy of Certified Social Workers (A.C.S.W.).
June 19, 1971	Ordained Deacon, Episcopal Diocese of Pennsylvania.
1972–1974	Lectured in homiletics and women's studies at the schools of the Episcopal Consortium for Theological Education in the Northeast.
July 29, 1974	One of the first eleven women to be ordained to the priesthood in the Episcopal Church, Philadelphia, Pennsylvania.
1975–1998	Assistant professor of pastoral theology at the Episcopal Divinity School, Cambridge, Massachusetts.
1988	Received an Honorary LLD from Regis College.
1994	Presented a woman for ordination in St. Paul's Cathedral at the Diocese of London's first ordination of women.
May 30, 2002	Died at Chilton House Hospice, Cambridge, Massachusetts.

Contents

Acknowledgments

These people made generous financial contributions toward the publication of this book: Anne Brewer, Carol Anne and Donald Brown, Ann Coburn, Mary Glasspool, Judy Holding, Brenda Husson, Jim Kowalski, Jean Hiatt Kramer, Lee McGee, Joanne Neel-Richard, Mary Anne Osborn, Margaret Rose, Katharine Jefferts Schori, Fredrica Harris Thompsett, Charles R. and Linda Tyson, and Susan Wyper. Without you, we could not have produced this volume of Sue Hiatt's speeches, sermons, and writings.

These colleagues contributed time and talent to helping us think about the content and shape of this book: Anne Brewer, Webb Brown, Alison Cheek, Ian Douglas, Mary Glasspool, Harvey Guthrie, Barbara C. Harris, Emily Hewitt, Jim Kowalski, Jean Hiatt Kramer, Robert Kramer, Jim Littrell, Lee McGee, Darlene O'Dell, and Ed Rodman. Your knowledge of Sue, and of what was important to her, was invaluable to us on this project.

Thanks to B.K. Hipsher for filming a conversation among Sue's friends in Brookline, Massachusetts, and for consulting with us.

Thanks to Susan Cannon, who kept track of the contributions being made to this effort through "the Hiatt Legacy Fund" at the Cathedral Church of Saint John the Divine.

Thanks to Gerry Azzata, who read, and helped Carter sort, these documents in 2006 when we were originally hoping to publish, but could not find a publisher. Gerry's careful reading and reflections, as a feminist who did not know Sue personally, was an important resource.

Thanks to Ruth Tonkiss Cameron and Betty Bolden at the Archives of Women in Theological Scholarship, The Burke Library of Columbia University, Union Theological Seminary, for patient guidance and assistance as we studied the Sue Hiatt collection over the past few years.

Thanks to Darlene O'Dell, beloved friend and colleague, who has been working alongside us on her own book, *The Story of the Philadelphia Eleven*, which will be published at the same time as this volume by Seabury Press.

Of course, many special thanks to Nancy Bryan, editorial director at Church Publishing Incorporated, who offered enthusiastic encouragement from the moment we consulted her in 2011 about the possibility of this publication.

Finally, we appreciate each other: Janine, for her sharp reading, and rereading, of Sue Hiatt's writings, and for her editorial abilities and willingness to work tirelessly on bringing this book project to fruition; Carter, Sue's courageous ally, for her creative drive and brilliant synthesis of Sue's selected writings. And we are immensely grateful for each other's good company and good humor as we worked together to bring to light Sue Hiatt's work.

As one of Sue's best friends and closest colleagues, Carter already knew why this book was so important. As a passionate (somewhat younger) feminist who did not know of Sue Hiatt but had heard of the "Philadelphia Eleven," Janine discovered why this book is worth a read by any woman who seriously wants to change the world or make a real difference in her own time and place.

Carter Heyward and Janine Lehane
September 15, 2013

Prologue

Carter Heyward

Once in a while, if we are lucky, we encounter someone of Sue Hiatt's stature. She was not only a brilliant community organizer, a fine scholar especially of women's history, a wise and compassionate pastor, and a much revered professor of feminist pastoral theology, she was a spiritual giant, and one of a kind. Like a massive green tree planted near water, Sue Hiatt's roots grew deep in our common sacred soil, her branches stretching wide and high to provide shelter and nutrition, safety and beauty, for countless women and men who came to her seeking justice and hope.

Those who recognize Sue Hiatt's name know her role as the leader of the movement for the ordination of women priests in the Episcopal Church, a struggle that led to the controversial "irregular" ordination in 1974 of eleven women, including Sue. It was Sue Hiatt's belief, as a savvy organizer, that the church would allow women's ordination only when it became harder not to ordain women than to ordain us. She reasoned that that this would come about only if the church were pressed hard from within by women who, refusing to accept the church's rejection, proceeded to be ordained prior to the church's authorization of our ordination. This was the strategy of the "Philadelphia Ordination"—to generate tension within the Episcopal Church that would have to be resolved sooner rather than later. The women who were ordained, the bishops who ordained us, and thousands of supporters, came together in the Philadelphia Ordination in order to push the church toward authorizing the ordination of women, which indeed it did two years later at its General Convention.

Today there are thousands of women priests throughout the Angli-can Communion, and dozens of women bishops. Behind this historic global achievement, the figure of Sue Hiatt looms large as one of its chief architects.* Without a doubt, she was the driving force behind the Philadelphia Ordination in the United States. Not only did she conceive of it as a strategy, she also believed passionately that the ordination of women was right and good. We cannot quite grasp Sue Hiatt's obses-sive pursuit of justice for women in the church unless we see how con-fidently she stood in the Spirit of radical justice-making that inheres in all struggles for a better world. Sue recognized this Spirit of justice, struggle, and hope as the Power which Jesus of Nazareth, and other holy men and women, have experienced as the One Living God, by whatever name. More than anything, Sue wanted to be faithful to this God.

A resounding consensus among all who were touched, and often changed, by her life is that Sue Hiatt was a beacon of faithfulness to God, and that her faithfulness was not only remarkable, it was instruc-tive and important to pass on. This then is the primary reason for a volume of Sue Hiatt's writings. The book might have been called *Faith: An Instructor's Manual*, or less personally, and closer to Sue's style, *Faithfulness: A Manifesto*. As it stands, its title, *The Spirit of the Lord Is Upon Me*, reflects Sue's reliance on the language of the Bible, with which she understood herself and couched her own vocation as a priest as well as her preaching and teaching. In Christian Scripture, these words are first spoken by the prophet Isaiah (61:1). Later they are quoted by Jesus, according to the physician-evangelist Luke (4:18). Jesus's use of Isaiah's radical proclamation that "the Spirit of the Lord" was upon him, igniting his speech and inspiring his message, set him squarely in the prophetic tradition of Israel. It is noteworthy that Sue Hiatt experienced her own mission as priest and teacher as steeped in the prophetic tradition in which Jesus himself was rooted.

Shortly before her death in 2002, Sue asked me to be executor of her writings, which she had organized in chronological order, though

* The global movement for women's ordination in the Anglican Communion benefitted from the shared leadership of dozens of strong, talented women such as Patricia Brennan and Diane Heath in Australia, Susan Adams in New Zealand, Monica Furlong and Ann Poad in England, and dedicated women elsewhere in Europe, the Americas, Asia and the Pacific, and Africa.

often in note rather than narrative form. She had wanted the public to understand her, not simply for her own sake, but for the sake of God's ongoing movement in the world. Sue hoped that her life and words might inspire folks to engage in the struggles for justice, and might help them figure out how to do it.

For more than ten years now, those who knew and loved Sue as an organizer for justice, teacher or colleague, friend or neighbor, priest in the church or hostess in her home, have asked that her work be made available to a wider public. An earlier effort to find a publisher for Sue's work failed, despite some fine editorial help from my feminist friend and neighbor in North Carolina, Gerry Azzata, whose work with Sue's papers in 2006 provided some useful organization for the book that is now in your hands. This time around, almost seven years later, our efforts to find a publisher led us fortuitously to Nancy Bryan, editorial director at Church Publishing Incorporated. With Nancy's encouragement, Janine Lehane and I have selected for this book some two dozen pieces by Sue Hiatt—essays, lectures, and homilies that span almost fifty years.

The earliest papers were written while Sue was in high school, and they include her thoughts about "woman as domestic animal" (1953). This senior honors paper marks "Suzy," at seventeen years of age, as, perhaps, one of the earliest, youngest, smartest, and most uppity feminists of our generation. May her precocious young self be remembered and praised! May Suzy Hiatt spark hope, anger, and inspiration among today's teenage girls and young women who continue to face contemptuous, patronizing actions and attitudes from certain self-righteous, sexist politicians and patriarchal prelates.

Were she here, I can only imagine what Sue Hiatt would say about the mounting assaults on women's reproductive freedom throughout the United States and elsewhere. I can only guess her horror at the widening gap between rich and poor throughout the world which, as Sue knew and taught and preached at every opportunity, always hits women and children first and with the most devastating consequences. Young Malala Yousafzai of Pakistan would be among Sue's most hallowed heroes today. And could it be also that Sue's own bold spirit is infusing Malala's life and work in this world at this time?

A Complex, Paradoxical Prophet

Our companions at the Episcopal Divinity School in Cambridge, Massachusetts, where Sue and I were faculty colleagues for thirty years, and our friends in the ordination struggle and elsewhere in life, have urged me to be as honest as possible here about Sue so that, as our histories unfold, subsequent generations of activists—especially women—might better realize that our leaders are not "saints" in any simple sense. In many ways, Sue Hiatt embodied paradox. On the surface, her ways of being in the world seemed contradictory.

Sue was confrontational toward bishops and others in authority whenever she experienced them as upholding unjust laws or supporting the ongoing oppression of women or any other group traditionally marginalized in church and society. She did not mince words and she really did not personally care for many of these people, most often men wielding power over women's lives. She didn't care whether or not such men might be lovely individuals, kind and caring to their families, friends, and parishioners. If Sue had reason to believe they were participating, even passively, in oppressing or hurting women, gays, people of color, or poor people, she didn't wanted much to do with them personally. Her disdain for such people was camouflaged by her characteristically gentle and very kind demeanor. She was brilliantly able to distinguish, in relationships, between her own feelings and her behavior. This allowed Sue to work with grace and dignity alongside many people she didn't much care for in order to get the task done—ordaining women, planning conferences, teaching classes, etc. The key to her feelings toward others was *always*, for Sue, how seriously committed she perceived them to be to the liberation of women and other marginalized people.

She was characteristically soft-spoken, even when angry. Over the years of our friendship, during which we sat in the same faculty meetings, attended the same church events, marched in the same demonstrations, and often had our evening meals together, I don't recall ever hearing Sue raise her voice. Once in a blue moon, she might have uttered a four-letter word under her breath, but I doubt that many of her friends, much less her adversaries, ever heard such a word pass her lips.

There probably has never been a more radical feminist in church or society, in this or any culture, than Sue Hiatt in that she was constantly on alert for signs of any violence against women, institutional or interpersonal. Moreover, she understood all violence against women to be connected through the same insidious historical networks spawned by patriarchal religion. Not only was Sue quick to point out ways in which the church was not taking women seriously—for example, whenever competent women seminary graduates were being passed over for jobs—but also she was carefully attuned to how women students and other church women, lay and ordained, were being treated in their own homes.

At the same time, Sue was more conventional than many Christian feminist religious leaders in both personal style and in the substance of her theological interests and participation among feminists. Not only was she more "ladylike" in public than most other women of her generation, feminist or not, Sue was never especially interested in feminist liberation or womanist theologies or in being involved in networks of feminist and womanist theologians. This puzzled many of her feminist and womanist colleagues and students who couldn't figure out what made Sue tick.

On the one hand, they knew that no one was a more reliable ally in struggles against sexism in the church; they knew—because Sue had taught them—that all effective movements are collective, and they also knew that Sue was among the very best community organizers. After all, look at what she had brought into being in the Philadelphia Ordination and a year later in the Washington Ordination that served strategically to underscore the power of the movement that had surfaced in Philadelphia. Sue's students and colleagues knew her to be radically communitarian in her understanding of what makes lasting social change.

On the other hand, Sue often seemed to be a loner, a woman who kept to herself much of the time, someone who did not attend feminist conferences or gatherings if she could help it because she found them to be tedious. As one of Sue's closest friends, I came to understand this apparent contradiction as a paradox. She was a strong, tenacious feminist woman who was passionate about justice for women and who was also personally reserved, often rather muted, in the presence of other strong women. She used words sparingly and did not like lots of argument, particularly if she found it primarily abstract or academic. Though brilliant herself, and an astute historical thinker, Sue was not an academic feminist theologian and was not particularly knowledgeable of, or concerned about, feminist theology or feminist theory. Her interests as teacher and priest were in the practice of ministry, the actual day-to-day issues and challenges facing women.

When I first met Sue in Alexandria, Virginia, in 1971, at a conference on women's ordination, it was clear to me that Sue took her sisters seriously and respected the diversity of our gifts and talents. During the ordination struggle and when we became colleagues at the Episcopal Divinity School in 1975, I never doubted the trustworthiness of our relationship as feminist priests, activists, teachers, colleagues, and theologians. Our styles were different. Sue had her work, I had mine, and we trusted and valued each other's contributions to our common goal as priests and teachers: strengthening the fabric of our students' lives, especially our women students, our gay and lesbian students, our African-American and other students of color, and the lives of our white male students who were committed to putting justice work at the heart of their vocations.

Some of our critics complained that "Sue shows so little interest in feminist liberation theology," and that "Carter doesn't seem to care much about the practice of ministry." Occasionally, Sue and I would feel some aggravation at each other's ways of living our vocations. But we respected each other with an unshakable and shared loyalty. I regarded Sue's muted support for my work as a feminist liberation theologian as a reflection of her personal reserve. I had realized increasingly, over the years, that Sue needed to conserve her own strength for the work that she had chosen to accomplish.

She did not, for example, care very much about inclusive language, whereas I did and still do. While Sue didn't like sexist language in liturgy, it was not a critical issue for her as it was for many of us who decried the connections between patriarchal liturgical language and the ongoing oppression and trivialization of women. Like most of the first women priests and many other ministers, men as well as women, Sue would simply change the language to make it more inclusive as she preached and led worship.

More important to Sue, in terms of her own talents and energies, was that women be well educated to help lead the church, either as lay or ordained, and that qualified women be able to be ordained, hired as priests, and consecrated as bishops. For example, in 1988, fourteen years after the Philadelphia Ordination, Sue was delighted to facilitate the election of her friend Barbara C. Harris as the first Episcopal woman bishop in the United States and the first Anglican woman bishop in the world. These efforts, not feminist theology as an academic subject and not liturgical language, were Sue's priority—to secure the ordination of women as priests and bishops and to do everything in her power to provide encouragement to women seeking to serve the church as ordained or lay ministers, depending upon their "calls" (their own sense of what God, as they understood God, was "calling" them to do). This is why Sue was renowned throughout the last half of her life as "bishop to the women." Women and men throughout both the U.S. Episcopal Church and the global Anglican Communion often looked first to Sue Hiatt for guidance whenever a particular woman's vocation was at stake.

A paradox for which Sue was well-known, even celebrated, throughout her life, was the tension between her pessimism and the twinkle in her eye. Sue's friends referred to her affectionately as "Eeyore" or as "Cassandra"—the one who sees a problem under every rock, and who comes with bad news. A colleague famously remarked, "Sue always expects the worst to happen—and she's usually right." Sometimes the best would happen—as when Barbara Harris was elected bishop—in which case Sue would register delight, and surprise! In all cases, even when being her pessimistic self ("It's all the same at the bottom of the river"), Sue's eyes would twinkle in the direction of whomever she knew understood what she meant. It was as if Sue was always saying to her allies, "You know, things are bad, but we've got each other, and so on we go. Don't worry, it'll be all right—if not good."

She often had a quip ready to drop on the spot if needed, such as when she stood up in a meeting between eight or ten women and some bishops in New York City who were undecided about ordaining us and simply said, "Okay, sisters, let's vote with our feet!" Up we got and out we walked, confounding the bishops, and contributing momentum toward women's ordination. (Those who are especially interested in the paradoxes inherent in Sue's person will find more in the section called "Remembering Sue" of this volume, especially in the pieces by Barbara Harris, Margaret Kramer, and me, as well as notes from the meetings at Chilton House Hospice and with Bishop DeWitt.)

Who Should Read This Book?

From several hundred pages of notes and narrative left by Sue Hiatt, Janine and I have attempted to compile a selection that sheds light on her legacy as the chief architect of women's ordination in the Anglican Communion and, as such, one of the leading figures among women in religion in the last half of the twentieth century in Western Christianity. That her name is not a "household word," as one of the publishers who earlier rejected these pieces lamented, is hardly surprising, given how fast we forget the lives and legacies of women who have gone before us in patriarchal Christian history.

Obviously this is a book for anyone interested in women's history, women's religious history, modern church history, the history of the Episcopal Church USA and the Anglican Communion, as well as those interested in strategies for social change, especially in religious organizations. Students and scholars in these areas will find this volume useful.

But there is another group of prospective readers to whom I especially commend this book. At a 2006 conference of several hundred Episcopal women priests in the United States, those of us who had been involved in the struggle for ordination were told by some of the younger women priests that sexism is no longer an issue, at least not a major one, and that they do not share our concerns, much less our anger. I imagined Sue Hiatt shaking her head, mumbling something, and turning her twinkling eyes on us "oldies." I hope that many of the younger generations of women priests, some of them now approaching their own retirement, will take an interest in finding out about the woman whose efforts put them where they are. I would hope that their daughters, nieces, granddaughters, and their sons and grandsons too, might find these pieces instructive. For in these pages there is much to learn about the power of faith and the importance of strategy in every serious endeavor to bring about social change, whether in religious organizations or elsewhere in our life together on this planet. There is also much to be said for learning that we ourselves did not simply "happen" into our lives and work. Others made it possible for us to come along. The more we learn about this, the more compelling our own legacies are likely to become.

Readers will find many of these pieces inspirational, or just plain interesting as historical documents. There is a lot of good humor in them, and a great deal of wisdom. Had Sue herself been more interested in feminist biblical interpretation, she might have seen herself more clearly as a living, breathing incarnation of the Divine Sophia/Wisdom, because that is, I believe, who she was. Or perhaps Sue did realize this and chose not to mention it.

C.H.

In part two, we have retained fidelity to the original text of "The Domestic Animal" (December 1953) by recording bibliographical information as Sue wrote it. We have inserted bridging notes written by Sue, either intact or with our minor additions for the purposes of clarity, between the major sections of this volume. Sue organized her ideas in note form in a particular way when preparing sermons, speeches, and essays. She elaborated on these notes when she preached. These notes give the reader the essence of Sue's thinking on a specific topic or issue and they are essential to her writing process. We are hopeful that these bridging notes will spark readers' interest in undertaking serious biographical work on Sue Hiatt and others who pioneered women's ordination and who shaped women's history.

J.L.

PART ONE

THE RADICAL
LADY WHO CHANGED
THE CHURCH

Introduction to Part One
The Radical Lady Who Changed the Church

If you read only one essay in this book, this should be it. Initially a speech to the Ecumenical Conference on Women's Ministries at Graymoor Conference Center, Garrison, New York, in March 1983, this piece carries the reader into the core of Sue Hiatt's passion for justice for women and her strategic intelligence about how to make it happen—in this case the ordination of women priests—in one relatively small organization, the Episcopal Church in the United States. This essay is a case study in community organizing. It is also a manifesto in feminist pastoral theology, which might be defined as reflections on God in ways that strengthen women, thereby contributing to the healing of their wounds and to their refusal to make peace with their own oppression.

Hiatt contends here that women must "take" authority, rather than wait to have it bestowed upon us, if significant change is to be brought about in realms of gender equality. She speaks both politically, about how social change generally happens, and personally, about her own vocation: "I realized . . . my vocation was not to continue to ask for permission to be a priest, but to *be* a priest." This sensibility is present early in Hiatt's own life. The theme of her high school honors paper (see part two, "The Domestic Animal") is that women need to take responsibility for our own lives, and assume authority for and insist upon the conditions in which we will live. Sue Hiatt has little use for women whining about, or resigning ourselves passively to, sexist behavior on the part of individuals or society. If you don't like it, do something about it, is her mantra.

She is cool and strategic in sorting out the relationships in which she and the other feminist women activists found ourselves in the 1970s. Referring to the bishops who wanted to ordain women but felt, for various reasons, that they couldn't take this step as quickly as we were demanding, Sue Hiatt writes, "They were our friends and allies but, since they could go no further, we had to go on without them." She did not hesitate to lead women deacons out of a meeting in New York City in 1973 with these very bishops, our "friends and allies," by commanding in her soft, understated way, "Sisters, let's vote with our feet!" So out we walked, leaving behind the men who, until then, had perceived themselves as our best hope. In that moment, the women deacons and our bishops realized that *we women were our own best hope.*

Hiatt concludes this essay, which should be required reading for women and men who intend to bring about social change in the church, academy, or elsewhere, with four "principles" for organizing:

1. Women, or others who seek social change that will affect them in a primary way, must take a primary role in bringing that change about. Women are their own best advocates and they have no reason to apologize for this. In fact, it should make us proud to be women—and to be advocates for ourselves and our sisters.

2. We must learn how the institutions that we wish to change actually work and how best to influence them. This is the basis of good strategy, which was one of Sue's special gifts as a social worker trained in community organizing.

3. We women must be united and avoid horizontal violence—that is, we must avoid sniping at other women with whom we may have different strategies but with whom we share long-term goals. More than anything, we must avoid blaming women for sexist oppression and violence against women. At the same time we must hold women responsible for struggling together against such oppression and violence.

4. Specifically in relation to the church, we women must remember that the church needs us. Later in life, Hiatt would add, ". . . more than we need the church." Implicit in her life and

work, throughout this essay and this book, is Sue Hiatt's belief that women could live strong, creative, spiritually rich lives without the church—and would do better without the church than to continue to submit ourselves to the church's oppression and its trivialization of women.

C.H.

How We Brought the Good News from Graymoor to Minneapolis

An Episcopal Paradigm

Journal of Ecumenical Studies 20, no. 4 (Fall 1983): 576–84

When I was asked to speak at this conference, I accepted the invitation immediately and enthusiastically. The time was right, I felt, to tell the story of women's battle for ordination in the Episcopal Church. Women are good at telling stories, but we are less good at learning from those stories, and not good at all at recalling and cherishing our own history (even when we call it "herstory"). So I have a story to tell—a history to recapture. I hope we can all learn from the recalling of these events.

You probably know that women may serve in all orders of ministry in the Episcopal Church and that the Episcopal Church is the United States manifestation of the worldwide Anglican Communion. You may remember that in the summer of 1974, in Philadelphia, three retired and resigned Episcopal bishops ordained eleven women deacons to the priesthood without the consent of the bishops under whom the women served or the consent of the church at large. You may also remember that in September 1976, the Episcopal Church in general convention in Minneapolis voted approval for the ordination of women to the priesthood. Women began to be ordained regularly and legally in January 1977. It is these events and the actions of churchwomen leading up to them which I recall here.

In the prayerbook ordination service according to which I was ordained priest in July 1974, the bishop in laying hands on the head of the ordinand recites this formula: "Take thou authority to execute the office of a Priest in the Church of God, now committed to thee by the imposition of our hands." I had often pondered that transfer of authority when I attended ordinations. The bishop does not confer priestly authority but simply tells the ordinand to assume it. The story of the ordination of women priests in the Episcopal Church is a case study of women "taking" authority, and that is what is instructive about it. Somehow over the past fifteen years women in my church (and in many of your churches and synagogues as well) were able to take the initiative and to change institutions not noted for their susceptibility to change. The details vary with the struggles, but women's taking the initiative and stepping away from our time-honored position of supplicant is what has changed about women vis-à-vis the church.

Beginning at Graymoor

The story of women's taking authority in the Episcopal Church began at Graymoor in April 1970. If I had to pick a moment it would be the sharing of an agapé (since of course none of us were priests or even deacons at that time) on Orthodox Easter. On that bright April morning about sixty Episcopal women gathered out on the lawn to close a two-day conference and to strengthen our resolve to insist on the opening of all aspects of the church's ministry to women. The conference had grown out of the secular women's movement, which was itself beginning to grow out of the anti-racist and peace movements of the late 1960s. In fact, the conference had been organized by women active in the Episcopal Peace Fellowship who simply sent out a call to all women on their mailing list to come together to discuss the church's discrimination against women.

It was a difficult conference, as it had attracted a very diverse group of women. There were young militant feminists who felt peripherally connected to the church but very wounded by it. There were seminary-educated women of all ages, many of whom had never found fulfilling ministries within the church. There were laywomen just barely hanging on, and nuns and clergy wives who felt trapped and exploited by the institutional church. A few of the women had owned their own vocations to priesthood.

We fought and talked and cried together for two days and finally came up with "the Graymoor Resolution" in which we branded the institutional Episcopal Church "racist, militaristic and sexist. Its basic influence on our own lives is negative." We resolved further "that women as well as men [must] be accepted and recognized as equals so that they may function in proportion to their numbers in all aspects of the Church's life and ministry, including but not limited to . . ." and here we listed every office in the church we could think of, from vestries to altar guilds and from bishops to thurifers. We agreed on the final wording and signed the document in the course of that Easter agapé.

The Graymoor meeting did not lead directly to further organizational activity. The resolution was distributed and widely publicized, but no follow-up meetings were arranged, nor was an organization begun. But women began to take authority at Graymoor thirteen years ago simply by meeting together as women and sharing with other women what we had all been thinking privately for some time. We began to connect—to meet and know each other and to affirm ourselves as sisters.

The Episcopal Church meets in General Convention every three years, and such a convention was coming up in October 1970. The 1967 convention had appointed a commission on ordained and licensed ministries to look into the matter of women's ministries, but no one at church headquarters had gotten around to convening it. In May and June of 1970, some of the Graymoor veterans discovered that the commission was made up of people who, if they met, would most likely propose that women be ordained to all orders of ministry. We persuaded them to meet rather than report "no progress" as headquarters had requested, and, after a September meeting, they came to the convention in Houston with such a resolution. In addition, four women came to that October convention to discuss our call to priesthood. With the help of some experienced church politicians and publicists (male clergy), the women and the commission recommendation caught the interest of the convention. In fact, the resolution to ordain women was debated and voted on—winning the approval of a majority of clerical and lay delegates, but losing by a narrow margin in the clergy order due to the technicalities of how the votes are counted.

The issue of women's equality engaged many women at the convention, and on the morning after the defeat of the ordination resolution about fifty women crowded into a small hotel room to caucus on our response. The response was angry and forceful. Women had just been seated as lay delegates after a twenty-five-year debate and the church was congratulating itself on that, when suddenly the women were no longer grateful but turned hostile. The result of the women's anger was the last-minute approval by the convention of the ordination of women to the diaconate on the same basis as men. Over the next few years women seminary graduates began to be ordained as deacons.

Doing Things Decently and in Order

In April 1971, I took a trip through the Midwest to test the waters on whether Episcopal women might be organized to press for the full ordination of women. I was a trained, experienced community organizer, having worked for several years for the Philadelphia Welfare Rights Organization. But, like most women, I knew nothing about church politics. As a professional I also knew that it was not a good idea for an organizer to work on an issue in which she has a deep personal stake (I was scheduled to be ordained deacon in June 1971). My talks with women in Detroit and St. Louis convinced me, however, that Episcopal women were ready to claim their place in the church and that someone with the skills to help them do it would be a valuable catalyst.

For the next two years we worked to build a network and an organization to influence the 1973 convention to be held in Louisville, Kentucky. We enlisted sympathetic bishops, priests, and laymen, but the major work was done through the Episcopal Women's Caucus, organized at Alexandria, Virginia, on Halloween, 1971. Through regional branches the caucus researched and worked on the delegates to the upcoming convention. Organizing and educational events and meetings were held all over the country, and literature designed for varying levels of sophistication was produced. Again, with the help and advice of knowledgeable church politicians, we built a groundswell of enthusiasm for women's ordination.

But the opposition was also hard at work organizing a groundswell against such a plan. By the time the convention was held there were about forty women in deacon's orders (in addition to about seventy mostly elderly deaconesses who had been made deacons by the action of the 1970 convention). We were highly visible in clerical garb and on our best "winning of hearts and minds" behavior. This time the issue came as no surprise to the delegates, and they were cajoled and button-holed by both sides. When the vote finally came, women's ordination lost again. Again there was a majority of delegates voting yes, but this time the motion lost on the same technicality in both the clergy and lay orders.

By now the ordination of women was no longer a simple matter of equity that people had not thought about before, but a full-blown political issue threatening to "split the church." In 1973, most delegates were faced with the decision of whether it would be more trouble for the church to ordain or not to ordain women, and they decided it would be more trouble to do it. In 1976, when faced with the same question, the delegates decided it would mean more trouble not to do it. How the atmosphere changed so dramatically is the story of women at work in the intervening three years.

Moving Toward Irregular Ordination

Even before the Louisville convention had adjourned, a group of women and bishops had met to talk about "irregular" ordination of women to the priesthood. The meeting was not a happy one, as several bishops and a few women had come to dissuade the others. Some of us, how-ever, had felt a growing urgency in our vocations and had been increas-ingly aware that dramatic action was needed to break the logjam.

As early as 1965, I remember joking with a seminary classmate about his becoming a bishop and laying hands on me "suddenly." As late as the spring of 1973, I had had a conversation with J. A. T. Rob-inson, an English bishop, in which we had agreed that the only way women's ordination would come to the Church of England would be for a bishop or bishops simply to proceed to ordain a woman. After the defeat in Louisville, I had run into an older woman friend wise in the ways of the church who had remarked that she guessed the ordination of women would now become a perennial issue for general conven-tions, just as allowing women to vote as delegates had been from 1946 to 1970. Instantly I realized she was right and that my vocation was not to continue to ask for permission to be a priest, but to *be* a priest.

After the convention an increasing number of women began to feel as I did. In November at a conference of women we watched as young women seminarians were told by (male) church politicians to be polite and patient and to "let us do it for you girls." Later in November a small group of us met with our bishops to discuss next steps. They wanted to ordain us but feared the consequences. When they could not bring themselves to agree to proceed by a certain date, the women deacons walked out on them. That came as a shock both to them and to us, but it was a crucial step in our claiming of our own authority. These were our friends and allies, but since they could go no further we had to go on without them.

In December 1973, five of the deacons who had been at that meeting presented themselves for ordination at their diocese's annual priestly ordination. They went through the whole ceremony—took the vows and made a statement when the bishop asked (as is provided for in the service) for objections. When the bishop finally refused to lay hands on them, they walked out, taking with them about a third of the congregation, including the bishop's chaplain. In January 1974, another demonstration was held at a service where the Archbishop of Canterbury was the principal celebrant. That time two other bishops joined the women in their silent protest.

By early spring of 1974, an increasing number of women deacons were becoming restless and discouraged. In February the Presiding Bishop met with a delegation of women deacons and made it clear he would do nothing to further the priestly ordination of women. That same month one of the bishops most deeply committed to women's ordination died suddenly. Those of us who were willing to move ahead with an "irregular" ordination began to feel hopeless. We knew we needed bishops, and we had some strong supporters among the bishops, but none of them felt strongly enough committed to take the necessary risks.

Then, within the space of ten days in June, things fell into place and the long-discussed "irregular" ordination was in the planning stage. On Thursday, June 6, 1974, the Dean of the Episcopal seminary in Cambridge, preaching at graduation, announced that he would resign unless the school hired an ordained Anglican woman immediately for its faculty. He pointed out that many of the current students were women called to ordination, and they needed role models. The following Sunday a trustee of that seminary, the highest-ranking layman in the Episcopal Church, preached a sermon at a church in Syracuse, New York, in which he called for the immediate ordination of women priests by any brave bishops who could be found. The next Saturday at a service of ordination to the diaconate, the Dean of the Episcopal Seminary in Philadelphia also called for the immediate ordination of women to the priesthood. That evening he met with a bishop and a woman deacon to plan the when and where—no longer the whether—of an "irregular" ordination.

As that small group began contacting others for a planning meeting to be held in July, it became clear that the years of networking, strategizing, and discussing the issue had come to fruition. One bishop had written the organizing bishop in April that he "had crossed the Rubicon or the Jabbock or whatever," and he agreed to be part of an ordination as soon as possible. Another bishop had participated in the January demonstration, and he, too, readily agreed to come. Priests and laypersons contacted by the seminary dean were eager and excited. Women deacons agreed without hesitation, but with a certain practiced sense of disbelief that such an event might actually happen.

On July 10th a self-constituted planning group (five bishops, seven priests, six deacons, and four laypersons) meeting in Ambler, Pennsylvania, agreed to participate in an ordination to be held on the feast of Sts. Mary and Martha of Bethany (July 29) at a predominantly Black church in North Philadelphia. This parish church, the Church of the Advocate, was the home parish of one of the ordinands, and the invitation was extended by the Rector and vestry. How that event was planned and the details of it are another story in themselves. There was much uproar when the news of the plans leaked out—many threats and much heavy rhetoric. In the end it turned out to be a Spirit-filled occasion, with three retired and resigned bishops ordaining eleven women deacons to the priesthood amid a congregation of two thousand enthusiastic supporters. A fourth bishop, a diocesan, participated but did not ordain anyone himself.

Theologians would call that event an experience of *kairos*—all the preparations and longings of a great many people coming together in God's time, not ours. It had a "time out of time" feeling about it. Four years and more of women's bonding and taking control of our own lives culminated that hot July morning when the bishops told the women to take authority as priests in the church of God.

In retrospect, to have been ordained "irregularly" is the only way for women to have done it. Our ordination was on our terms, not the church's terms. We saw ourselves as deacons proceeding in obedience to the insistence of the Holy Spirit that the step be taken for the integrity of the church. Women were able, through much pain and hard work and witnessing, to bring bishops and clergy and laity to share our vision of a church in which (as the banner hanging on the altar at the Church of the Advocate that morning read) "In Christ there is neither male nor female, bond nor free, Jew nor Gentile—We are one."

Crime and Punishment

Of course, as we had anticipated, the institutional church was very angry. The bishops met in emergency session in Chicago in mid-August to decide what to do about us. Most of the eleven were present, and, despite the bishops' anger, there was a new tone in our dealings with them. The old threats were no longer effective because the struggle had moved to a new plane. When bishops called us by our first names, we responded by calling them by their first names. The relationship of lord and suppliant symbolized in that small matter was broken forever.

The way the bishops chose to deal with us was to resolve that no ordination had occurred on July 29th, and that we were still only deacons. That posture was so theologically indefensible (though they have never backed down from it) that most of us felt our only recourse was to start ministering as priests wherever and whenever we were asked to do so. We had refrained from priestly ministry up to that point in order to give the bishops a chance to respond, but when their response was so intransigent we felt we had no choice.

Over the course of the next eighteen months a number of things happened to keep the issue alive. The media had been much taken with events in the Episcopal Church. We became the "lighter side" of the news during Nixon's last days in August. When the bishops escalated the conflict, the media was eager to keep track of our tribulations.

In 1975, two male priests were tried and convicted in ecclesiastical courts of disobeying their bishops' "Godly admonitions" by inviting women priests to celebrate communion in their parish churches. Numerous other priests invited us to do the same thing, and we exercised our ministry as priests in a number of settings. Several of the women were "admonished" or "suspended," but the church avoided bringing us or the ordaining bishops to trial, because it did not want to argue about the validity of the ordinations in ecclesiastical court. Nor did it want the media to take it apart yet again as persecutors of women.

Meanwhile, the debate on whether women should or could be priests raged on as the church prepared for another General Convention. In September 1975, four more women deacons were ordained priests by another resigned bishop in Washington, DC. That ordination signaled to the church that "irregular" ordinations were likely to continue happening as women with priestly vocations continued to come forward. When the convention met in Minneapolis in September 1976, the delegates decided that it would be more trouble not to ordain women, given all the chaos of the last two years. They voted to ordain women to the priesthood beginning January 1977. The bishops tried to insist that the fifteen women who were already priests undergo "conditional ordination." The rest of the convention persuaded them, however, for the sake of peace, simply to recognize and "regularize" those previous ordinations.

The Present Situation

Now, nearly ten years later, there are over 600 clergywomen in the Episcopal Church—about 400 priests and 200 deacons. The history I have related is not widely remembered. Having finally accepted the ministry of women (though there are dioceses where women priests still are not recognized or accepted), the church, like most institutions, prefers to recall itself as welcoming the idea as soon as it was proposed. Clergywomen in most places are fairly well assimilated into the life of the church, and about thirty are even rectors of parishes.

In spite of the church's efforts to forget the late unpleasantness, I still take comfort in the fact that the ordination of women in the Episcopal Church came as a result of women's insisting on it—forcefully and skillfully. A sister priest reported to me last summer, after visiting with some Canadian women priests, that she found that our different histories affect very much where we are in our respective churches. The struggle in Canada was much less bitter. They began ordaining women legally and in an orderly fashion in 1976. My friend remarked that she finally realized why the Canadians were so timid in confronting their bishops. They had accepted ordination as a gift, whereas we had claimed it as a right. We stopped being grateful in 1970, and that made all the difference in terms of our self-imaging.

What We Have Learned

This story is a very specific instance of how the ordination battle was won. It is peculiar to the Episcopal Church in the United States. The bishops and women who will make it happen as Bishop Robinson predicted in the Church of England have yet to come forward. The other churches in the Anglican Communion which have women priests (there are no women bishops in the Anglican Communion as yet [in 1983])—Hong Kong, Canada, New Zealand, and Kenya—have all arrived there by different routes, and their women have different stories to tell. But I think there are principles about women's being heard in the institutional church which our story illustrates. Those principles might be helpful to women facing similar struggles.

First, if women want changes, we must insist on them and take the primary role in bringing them about. We cannot rely on the good will of our brothers—the changes we seek are seen as too trivial or too threatening, and they have no reason to work for them unless we insist. Of course, male allies are indispensible, but the initiative and the follow-up must be ours. The New Testament provides an inspiring role model in the importunate widow.

Second, we must learn how the institution works and how best to influence it. There is no substitute for accurate and complete information on how things work and the skills to make them work our way. Women in the fight for the Equal Rights Amendment are just now learning those facts of political life. We must also learn about the institutions we hope to change. Sometimes we will have to be unpleasant, but we should be able to do that with the wisdom of serpents.

Third, women must be united among ourselves and committed to our vision of the church as a safe and comforting place for all people. Our vision of cooperation and caring must start with our sisters, and we must be firm in our concern for them. Unless we can be as gentle as doves, there is no point in making any changes at all.

Finally, we must always remember that the church needs us and the insights and vision we bring. We did not do what we did in the Episcopal Church "only to annoy, because we know it teases." Those of us who fought for women's ordination did so because we thought the Gospel required it. A priesthood of men only could no longer adequately represent either Christ or humanity.

That same ordinal that charged me as a priest to take authority charged me as a deacon to "bring the needs of the world to the church." It was that part of my diaconal vows which I felt I was exercising in Philadelphia on the feast of Mary and Martha in 1974. The world was saying women are human, and we deacons felt the church needed to hear that message. Ten years later the message still needs to be heard. Because I am still a deacon, I still try to make my church hear. The good news has been brought from Graymoor to Minneapolis and is still traveling.

Notes: Reasons for Choosing the Ministry[1]

1st of Bishops questions to ordained:

"Do you think in your heart, that you are truly called . . . to the order and ministry of priesthood?"

A I think it

Reasons for choosing the ministry

It chose me—or rather H.S. has been after me for many years.
e.g., 8th grade—Jesus changed woman's lot—revolutionized it—interesting, but not much evidence in my church—

   post college—pastoral call by rector—nothing doing on the DRE
      bit
   St. Giles Cathedral—again I said no—
   1 year later on 25th birthday entered seminary—felt God would
      provide
   So that's how I got here—do feel truly called + know other women
      who do—
   This is question for church (not for us women)—we simply say,
      here we are, send us—
   As I hear debate I feel strangely detached—

---

1. These are the kind of notes available to us in the Suzanne Hiatt Papers, 1963–1998, held in The Archives of Women in Theological Scholarship, The Burke Library at Union Theological Seminary, Columbia University Libraries, in New York. The notes may be of particular interest to the reader who may wish to pursue further research in the archives.

talking about me + my ministry—but debate really has no effect
on that—

   call is clear to me—I've asked church to help me test it—it's passed
every test of canons + preparation—for me + others—double #
women studying

   So now church can say yes or no—I hope it will say yes because I
think that's the way to be true to the Holy Spirit—

   Just hope church won't say "maybe" again—
I know how it feels on personal level to resist Spirit—to run from it—
even more powerful on corporate level.

▮ ▮ ▮

It is Mary who has chosen the better part; it is not to be taken
from her

   —verse that can't be accepted
   like camel thru eye of needle
   can't believe Mary has chosen better part

      Mary has a way of being commended by J + making
      others angry

         Martha here, Judas in John's acct of anointing
   but plain truth is Jesus commends Mary, not Martha

      One thing rather than many——too many of us try to please
      everybody

         act of will *not* to help w. dishes + miss conversation—
         "liberated" women try to add sitting at Jesus feet to
         everything else we do—
Mary had to choose better part, therefore, other things had to go
Takes courage to choose, esp if you have no supports from society
Courage comes in small ways as well as large e.g., General Con-
vention—who cares about women priests—courage to take the insults

PART TWO

THE MAKING OF A FEMINIST PRIEST

Introduction to Part Two
The Making of a Feminist Priest

In these pages we meet seventeen-year-old "Suzy" Hiatt, writing about "God" and presenting a senior honors thesis on "The Domestic Animal" [Woman] as well as a short piece on "What I Want from a College Education." This section of the book concludes with one of Sue Hiatt's sermons (homilies) at the Episcopal Theological School in Cambridge, preached while she was a student in 1964—a decade after her teenage pieces and a decade before the Philadelphia Ordination. This homily is likely to disarm and delight the reader.

It is hard to comprehend fully that a young girl was writing such papers sixty years ago—almost two decades before the "second wave" of the women's movement in the United States actually hit the scene in the late 1960s and 1970s. Keep in mind that the 1950s were Ozzie and Harriet's generation, a period of happy housewives and strong male breadwinners and a time in which social change had little space in our dominant social or political discourse. In this context, seventeen-year-old Suzy Hiatt was an anomaly, a girl with no use for dominant social and political ordering of women's lives. Moreover, she was even at such a young age an unusually astute historian, already aware that change happens in history—and that it rests in the hands of those whose lives will be most transformed by it. In other words, she believed that women must take responsibility for their own liberation.

We see something else in young Sue Hiatt as she wrestles with her own life and where she is going—a strong degree of self-criticism which must have been steeped in self-reflection. Suzy is hard on herself, even as she insists that she must learn to be "patient and tolerant" with people of all kinds, including "super-intellectuals who are slightly unbalanced" and "pseudo-intellectuals [who] annoy me more than any other type." She writes: "What I want out of college . . . can only be achieved if I can correct the deficiencies in my own character. . . . I believe any corrections must come from me. My ability to live with and correct these things will spell the difference for me between a broad, liberal arts education and four wasted years." A decade later, as a seminarian in her late twenties, Sue Hiatt continues to be self-reflective. In her "Have Fun" homily, Hiatt suggests that self-contempt, rather than pride, may be our greatest sin. This bothers her, and she is committed to doing something about it in her own life. As in social change, so too in matters of personal change, for Sue Hiatt, those who seek change are responsible for doing something about it. She does not exempt herself.

This homily gives us a glimpse into the heart and soul of Sue Hiatt's theology as well as her own sense of vocation as a priest. She places herself—and all of us, ordained and lay—in the prophetic line of Jesus who quoted Isaiah as his own vocational springboard:

> The spirit of the Lord is upon me, because he has anointed me to bring good news to the poor. He has sent me to proclaim release to the captives and recovery of sight to the blind, to let the oppressed go free, to proclaim the year of the Lord's favor. (Luke 4:18–19)

Since we are *all* called by God to heed this call, it is not "arrogant" to insist that, in the struggles for justice, we are doing God's work. Our certainty that we are *together* in God grounds us in humility—that is, in a willingness to submit ourselves to God's movement for justice in history. For Hiatt, we Christians are "anointed by the same spirit to the same task," and we have the same responsibility. Whether we heed this common call is another matter. This question will provide the moral framework of Sue Hiatt's vocation as priest and community organizer. Throughout her ministry, she takes seriously her own responsibility to teach and preach our shared responsibility "to bring good news to the poor, proclaim release to the captives and recovery of sight to the blind, to let the oppressed go free."

In this part of the book, we move back with Sue Hiatt over sixty years into moments of a budding awareness, in which her passion for justice for women and her love of God as a "force for good" were taking hold. We also see here that, over a ten-year period, between the mid-1950s and mid-1960s, this intellectually gifted, self-reflective girl with a passion for women and a love of God has decided to plant herself with Jesus in the prophetic tradition.

C.H.

Suzy Hiatt
English XII
December 16, 1953

God

Through the ages, God has become less clearly defined in the minds of men. The Greek and Egyptian gods were definitely personalities; human beings possessed with divine powers. In the Greek gods, this divine power was all that separated god from men; the gods certainly did not have divine personalities, character or wisdom. Probably the early Greeks saw the evil in the world and were unable to correlate it to an omnipotent, all-good force. Hence they worshiped, out of fear, beings who caused more evil than good whenever they influenced human destiny.

During the middle ages, God remained a fearful giant, but his personality became less distinct. Christ had taught that God was love and truth, but the superstitious people again could not correlate the evil of the world and the goodness of God. Since they could not accept nor reject Christ's God, they made up hellfire and brimstone to show that God could be angry and vengeful. Hence God became an enigma and again out of fear the people worshiped him.

Today many people no longer consider God a personality. It is a supernatural force that created the world and controls its destiny. To me, God is the force of good in the world. There is not the slightest hint of anything malignant about God. My God cannot explain why there is evil in the world, nor does it attempt to. If I can go through life believing that somehow good, or God, will eventually triumph, I believe my faith will be as strong as or stronger than that of a man who has seen a celestial vision.

The Domestic Animal
by
Suzanne Hiatt
Northrop Collegiate School
December, 1953

Thesis: Although women in America gained political emancipation in 1920, they have not yet gained social and economic freedom, nor will they until social pressure, tradition and upbringing stop forcing them to conform to outmoded patterns of life.

Introduction: Unfortunately, the word feminist connotes an ax-swinging old fanatic. Women do not like to be labeled feminist, and thus learn to keep quiet about the injustices of their lives for fear of ridicule.

I. The upbringing and education of a girl have a lot to do with her ideas about her place in the world and help form her personality traits.

   A. Small girls are taught to play "house" and "mama." They can cry without being sissies while their brothers are taught not to cry.

   B. As they grow older they are expected to do household tasks that their brothers are excused from. Their morals are also more closely watched than those of their brothers.

   C. In contrast to her home life, her school life teaches a girl that she is the equal of any boy. In school she has complete equality with boys.

   D. The result of these two conflicting factors for many girls is confusion and uncertainty.

II. Most women marry and become housewives because they think there is no other course.

    A. Women can't hope to be promoted beyond a certain point in the business or political world.

        1. They are too apt to quit their jobs for marriage.

        2. They must compete against men with families to support.

        3. There is prejudice against women outside the home.

    B. It is far easier to take the security of a homebody than to try to fight society and a hostile world.

    C. Social pressure in many circles is very heavily against a girl who doesn't want to "settle down."

III. Women are chiefly to blame for their sex's being second best in America today.

    A. They create the social pressure and traditions which keep women at a level of mediocrity.

    B. They conform too easily.

    C. They do not fight or resist men because they do not want to lose what they suppose to be their "hold" over them.

Conclusion: Nothing can be done to improve woman's lot until woman herself does it. The picture does not seem hopeful because it is so very hard to change tradition. Perhaps in the distant future men and women can be treated as equals, but that time seems very far away.

The Domestic Animal

When I first told my mother that I was planning to write a term-paper on woman's place in society, she looked at me with a sardonic smile and asked if I planned to become a feminist. By feminist she meant, and the term is generally understood to mean, a completely irrational woman, carried away with the furor of the moment, chaining herself to the White House porch or hysterically screaming about the "tyrant man" as she fights off a policeman with her parasol.

Of course this is a ludicrous picture and naturally we laugh at the poor old soul, but unfortunately we tend also to laugh at the cause for which she fought as best she knows how. Let us look, then, for a moment at what she and her more rational sisters accomplished.

There are, in 1953, only twenty-seven countries in the world in which women are allowed to vote. In still fewer are they allowed to hold public office or enter the professions and, even in the United States, the most liberal country in the world, they are not constitutionally guaranteed the right to own property. Actually in no other country in the world are women as generally tolerated outside the home as they are in the United States. They can vote, hold public office, and work without any man's consent. Theoretically and legally they are completely independent in most states. Like it or not, admit it or not, we must attribute these comparatively great freedoms at least in part to the ax-swinging feminist of the early 1900s.[2]

As I have said, she is a ridiculous figure and has gotten more than her share of ridicule from members of both sexes. The memory of the feminist still seems to be embarrassing to women and they would just as soon forget about her. A modern feminist is met with tolerant smiles and gentle laughter from both men and women. Therefore the very idea of being labeled a feminist makes many women who are not satisfied with their lives and lots resign themselves to both and make the best of the situation. Before long they convince themselves that American women have no problems and anybody who thinks that they have is probably a frustrated feminist. This is, in general, the atti-

---

2. Ashley Montagu, *The Natural Superiority of Women*, pp. 22–23.

tude of American women today and until it improves the problem of "Women's place" can not be solved.

Even as small children, girls are taught their parents' idea concerning "women's place." In many homes, especially where there are children of both sexes, the tradition of the weaker sex is subtly and unconsciously transferred to little girls of three and four who, although they are as strong, active and intelligent as their brothers, are not encouraged to play the same games. They are taught from babyhood to play with dolls and doll houses. Little girl games consist mostly of playing "house," "mama" and "dress-up." When they become upset, little girls can cry and scream without their mothers telling them that they are acting "sissy-ish." A little girl learns at an early age that the best way to get something is to have a tantrum or pretend her feelings are hurt. She finds that adults consider it "cute" for her to "be in love" with one of the little boys with whom she plays. Unsuspecting parents attribute all this to "female temperament," never realizing that most of these female traits are natural human actions encouraged unnaturally in girls and discouraged in boys.

A little boy is taught to play with guns, trucks and other "boy's toys" while his sisters are holding tea-parties for their dolls.

> Somewhere in the home before even they go to school little boys learn to think that the superior male is tough and rough, and they struggle to form themselves on the model. I have actually heard American mothers tell their sons, "Don't be a sissy girl. You are a boy."[3]

Boys cannot cry or have tantrums without being told they are acting "like a girl." Many parents become embarrassed when their four-year-old boy prefers dolls to cowboy games and they do their best to develop "male" traits in him. From earliest childhood a boy's life is channeled into "male" and worldly pursuits while little girls, even though their parents do not push them as relentlessly as they push their brothers, are taught that they will ultimately become mothers and housewives.

---

3. Pearl Buck, *Of Men and Women*, p. 16.

As girls grow older, their lives are more obviously shaped to fit a place in the "female" world of the American home. They are taught by their mothers to make beds, cook meals, do dishes and generally "keep house." In many homes mother and daughter prepare dinner in the kitchen while father and son have "man to man" talks in the living-room. Boys are supposed to keep up with what's going on in the world while girls don't have to know anything about current events as long as they can pass in school and help with the housework at home. This is completely natural since the boys are being trained to live in the world while their sisters are being trained to live in the home.

In some homes girls hold a position slightly above that of a domestic, while boys, especially if there is only one son, hold a position slightly below that of a princeling. Of course the importance of the son is not exaggerated in all American families. But in most American families the daughters are being trained for the "career" of marriage while the sons are being trained to make their way in the hard, fast business world no matter what career they choose.

But just training girls to keep a home is not enough, it seems. They must also be taught, early in adolescence, to stay in the home and expect their husbands-to-be to protect them. Teen-age girls are more sheltered, more closely-watched and expected to be more chaste than the boys they associate with. If a teen-age girl becomes pregnant out of wed-lock, she is immediately and completely ostracized, if not by her friends at least by her friends' parents and all "self-respecting" people. But the boy who is responsible, if not left altogether blame-less, is at least left to carry on a normal life in normal society bothered by no more than an occasional black look or a whispered "boys will be boys you know." Even girls who are completely trusted and hence completely trust-worthy are required to be home at certain hours and never to stay home alone overnight. When they ask their mothers why they must follow outmoded patterns of life, they are usually met with the vague reply that "people will talk." Thus stupid and outdated tradition, which has shaped their lives from babyhood, at last rears its head openly and condemns them to an unnecessarily "sheltered" existence.

Perhaps this traditional course of events is accepted by most girls as natural and the matter is dropped at that. The unequal treatment of boys and girls would be fine if girls were kept in ignorance of how the male is taught. But in the American public school system, boys and girls are taught together. Thus they learn to value the same things, to attempt the same things and to understand and do the same things. All are treated alike and expected to follow the same school rules and to achieve the same scholastic betterment. American schools, especially high-schools and colleges, are, as far as scholastic achievement is concerned, the first and last stand of equality between the sexes. When women find out that they are as intelligent and capable as men, the idea of keeping them happy and contented as housewives becomes obsolete.

> The scheme which limits woman to homes should provide some means against her inheriting an intelligence equal to man's, which she does not need. If all women could be born with inferior minds and men with superior ones, the scheme of women for the home would doubtless be perfectly satisfactory. But unless that can be done, it is not satisfactory.[4]

With conflicting ideas of their role in life being thrust at them almost daily during the formative years, women often find themselves confused. They are discontented with the servitude of housework, but they have not been trained to have the confidence necessary for a career. At home they have learned that women should be dependent while at school they have learned that every person should be independent. At school they have learned that in America every person, regardless of color, religion or sex, has an equal opportunity, while at home they have learned that man is the breadwinner and woman's real happiness is in providing him with food and children. The idea of equality between the sexes is conversationally, legally and scientifically, a proven fact.

> There is no evidence that suggests women are naturally better at caring for children than men would be. In other words . . . there is even more reason for treating girls first as human beings and then as women.[5]

---

4. Buck, *op.cit.*, p. 25.

5. Margaret Mead, quoted by Elizabeth Bragdon in *Women Today*, p. 75.

But tradition cannot accept the evidence and girls are taught that this is all good and fine, but a girl cannot be happy without marriage and children. So women in America are confused by their educational training.

Unfortunately, this confusion is palled by the confusion confronted by a woman who has decided to believe what she has learned about equality and has set out to find a place for herself outside the home. Sooner or later the average or slightly above average woman finds the weight of opinion and circumstances too heavy for her to contend with, and is forced to retreat back into the home or into a profession generally conceded to be a "woman's field." There are too many black marks against a woman for her to overcome these circumstances without a Herculean effort which many men could not muster.

The first of these black marks is the fact that chances for advancement beyond a certain point in business or a profession are almost non-existent for women. In the first place, most business-men consider a woman a bad training risk because they never can tell when she will simply drop her job to get married. No one wants to spend years grooming a promising young woman for a responsible job only to see all his effort nullified by a simple marriage ceremony.

Many women who marry don't stop work immediately, but obviously if they are expected to keep house and have children they are no longer very interested in a career. "[Women] are the eternal amateurs and no professional . . . wants to work with amateurs. Their very attitude toward themselves and the job damn them to second-rateness."[6]

Secondly, they are competing against men who are absolutely required under our social system to be breadwinners and hold jobs. Naturally men resent women who, they think, should be at home, trying to gain a foothold outside of their "line." The employer will, and probably justifiably, give a promotion to a man who has a family to support over a woman who is expected to support only herself. "Women are not welcome outside the home except in subsidiary positions, doing, on the whole, things men do not want to do."[7]

---

6. I.A.R. Wylie, quoted by Elizabeth Bragdon, *op. cit.*, p. 23

7. Buck, *op. cit.*, p. 69.

But the biggest reason why women can't succeed outside of certain fields is the prejudice of the general population, half of whom are women themselves, against women in business. Despite a half-century of feminists and equal rights legislation, the mass of people still feel that "woman's place is in the home." Naturally employers, no matter how liberal they are, or political parties, no matter how sure they are that they will win, hesitate to endanger their public relations by promoting women beyond a certain point or backing them as candidates in big elections.

But why should a woman even attempt to buck this kind of prejudice? It certainly promises a much easier life to settle down at an early age and marry a good man. After she has had enough children to insure the carrying on of her husband's name and has gotten them safely through infancy, she can send them off to school each morning and have the whole day free until mid-afternoon. Housework is a relatively easy task and with modern conveniences it can be gotten down to a system requiring half a day's work. She has all day to do this half a day's work so why should she complain?

She has security and protection from the hard, cruel world and for many women this is all that is needed for a happy life. Thirty-eight per-cent of American women have children under eighteen. This leaves over thirty-five million women who could work but are either too afraid of the world of men to try it, or too lazy to care to try it.[8] Security has been their good in life and they have managed to stifle any ideas they ever may have had about independence in order to gain the security society offers to a woman who has legally become a wife and mother and thus assured man of a place to live and eat.

But if she can't see the security of marriage and the fact that she's not wanted in business, a young woman is in many cases gently but firmly reminded on almost any occasion that she "is getting along in years and that husbands are hard come by." Whenever anyone asks me what my sister, who is twenty-three and single, is doing, I anticipate three questions. They are: 1. Does she go out much? 2. Does she have

---

8. E. Lansing. "What More Do Women Want?" *Independent Women*, p. 123.

any special beaux? 3. Is it serious? My interrogators seldom disappoint me by not asking all of these questions.

"Yes" I answer to the first two questions, but when I say "I don't think so" to the third, a look of disappointment and pity comes over the face of the inquirer. To many people it is appalling that a girl who has been out of college for two years is not even engaged. I can almost hear them thinking ". . . and such a pretty girl too! My, my." Is it any wonder then that

> The emphasis on married happiness as the only form of successful adjustment possible for women has caused some single women to reject the pattern of single living and to refuse to adapt themselves to it?[9]

Social pressure may seem like a petty reason for giving up a career and settling down to the life of a homebody, but among women especially it can be applied so insidiously and constantly that it will break down the desire for independence of the strongest feminist. I think Margaret Mead expresses far better than I could the goal to which many women are steadily and ruthlessly pushed:

> If you are a man, your way of making a living is still a matter of choice; if you are a girl, it ultimately isn't. Good cooks, poor cooks, and no cooks at all, girls who from childhood have been "baby-carriage peekers" and girls who shudder at a child's shrieks . . . —all are expected, because they fall in love and want to be married, to want also to be homemakers and to enjoy the routine of bringing up children.[10]

It is not a very encouraging picture but very few people even consider women a minor problem in America today. Obviously men are never going to encourage them to leave the home; it is a man's world and they would just as soon it remained so. Women are the only ones who can improve woman's lot and their failure to do so is obvious from conditions today. Instead of using their independence, American

---

9. Ruth Reed, *The Single Woman*, p. 90.

10. Margaret Mead, quoted by Bragdon, *op. cit.*, p. 72.

women have done more to hinder it than any other force in American history. Let us re-examine the barriers to complete equality for women and see how this is true.

The first and most impregnable barrier is tradition. Tradition is the most insidious and elusive force working against ambitious women today. It cannot be pinned down, but it can be traced fairly generally to women themselves. Small children learn from their mothers what is expected of them because their fathers learned from their mothers that the care of small children is entrusted to women. It is human and natural for a woman to train her children as she was trained; thus the little girl becomes the straw-housewife; the little boy the straw-boss. Women are expected to marry and have babies and men are expected to work because that's the way things have always been. Women are expected to be loyal and true to their husbands while men are allowed to "sow a few wild oats" now and then without feeling any great repercussions.

Perhaps this tradition all started fifty thousand years ago when men first subdued woman by brute strength. Although men no longer go out to club a tiger for dinner because it is not necessary, women still stay at home to "protect the cave" regardless of the fact that the necessity of the act has long since vanished.

> The Bureau of Labor Statistics lists 20 million women, nearly half of all adult female Americans as essentially idle. . . . Many are over 40 and belong to a generation which frowned on work for any but poverty-stricken women. . . . They read too much low-grade fiction and escape too readily into dream realms of movies and soap operas.[11]

Having borne and raised the babies, the American woman considers her life's work finished and society encourages her in this belief. "Mother," although sloppy, lazy, and useless, is still a chauvinist symbol of America; secure in her place through over-emotional movies, radio, and newspaper drivel. Tradition expects her to rest on her laurels and live off "Dad" until they can retire together. It is tragically true that, in America—

---

11. "American Women's Dilemma," *Life*, p. 109.

We live under the pressure of institutions we did not create; we are obsessed by taboos and prejudices we have inherited as inexorably as we have inherited our skins. . . .[12]

Tradition then, founded and protected chiefly by women, becomes a more than ordinary force in every life. Very few escape its confines. As Thoreau so beautifully put it, "Shams and delusions are esteemed for soundest truths, while reality is fabulous."[13]

But why should women stand for the fetters of tradition and social pressure? They put up with them because they have been trained from childhood to take the line of least resistance. This training naturally leads them to conform easily. Women are prey to fashion designers because they have been taught to follow the crowd and stay in step. If Christian Dior says short skirts, the models begin to wear short skirts and soon everybody has chopped her hemline a good three inches. The sheep trait is evident in men too, but women who don't conform are dealt with far more coldly then men. Since women love to gossip, or rather assume that they must cultivate a love for gossip, a woman who "gets out of line" leaves herself wide-open to censure and criticism. Women, although they think more radically than men, tend to act more conservatively.[14] New ideas are wonderful but attempts to use them might lead to unpleasantness and most women would rather avoid unpleasantness.

"Nobody keeps them [women] back," the American man declares. Ah, nobody but everybody! For they are kept back by tradition expressed through the prejudices not only of men but of stupid, unthinking, tradition-bound women.[15]

These traditions must be conformed to before they have any effect. The American woman has shown through her apathetic use of the vote and other privileges, her willingness and apparent eagerness to conform.

---

12. Abraham Myerson, quoted by Bragdon, *op. cit.*, p. 310.

13. Henry Thoreau, *Walden*, p. 101.

14. Lloyd Morris, quoted by Bragdon, *op. cit.*, p. 331.

15. Buck, *op. cit.*, p. 62.

In addition to creating and conforming to tradition, woman has contributed to her servitude in still another way. In childhood a woman learns that she is a "mere auxiliary to a male rather than . . . an independent separate human being. Therefore she learns to gain her ends by making herself alluring, by serving as an inspiration, by being useful to some male or males."[16]

She learns about such men as Abraham Lincoln and James Madison with special emphasis given to the part played in their lives by Ann Rutledge and Dolly Madison. Her mother tells her that women run things behind the scenes by gently guiding and advising their sons and husbands. She is gradually led to believe that her role in life is to inspire some man to great heights of achievement and she becomes complacent to this idea.

But women are not generally taught confidence and so they become afraid to face up to the man they want to direct for fear they will lose their "hold" over him. Pearl Buck thinks, and I heartily agree, that this idea of woman's quiet but great influence over man is the American men's way of "kidding the little woman along." But until the American woman realizes this, she will vote the way her husband does and do whatever he expects her to do.

Since present society almost requires a woman to have a man, women will do almost anything to keep from losing their "hold" over men. Some of my own friends will go out with a boy even if it is extremely inconvenient, just to keep him from going out with another girl. Of course this is an adolescent course of action, but I believe that the trouble with many American women is that they never give themselves a chance to outgrow adolescence, nor are they generally expected to.

And so we have American women in a situation which they themselves created. A great many of them are confused about their place in life and what is expected of them. Legally, they have more rights than any other women in the world; actually they are hopelessly tangled in tradition and convention. All women, especially mothers who have raised daughters the same way they were raised, are to blame.

---

16. Lansing, *op. cit.*, p. 97.

We are between a period of great restriction for women and what may develop into a period of great freedom for them. It's entirely up to the female half of the population. If women would only give up the absurd idea that their place is at all times and under any conditions in the home and realize that they can contribute more to the world in which they live than children, they could be truly happy as they haven't been for centuries. Men no longer spend all their time fighting and hunting, why should women be fooled into thinking they must spend all their time cooking and caring for home and children. Home freezers and public schools have taken these jobs away from women and left them with nothing to do and very few ways to avoid doing nothing.

I am not optimistic about the future of women. Tradition is almost impossible to change unless all the women involved want to change it. This situation is almost as unlikely as to be proclaimed impossible.

When and if woman finally does tell tradition to go hang, she will at last live in a world of people, not just men. If she ever does, I only hope I can be reborn to live in the happy, balanced world she will create.

Bibliography

Text (Books)

Bragdon, Elizabeth, Editor. *Women Today*. New York: Bobbs, 1953.

Buck, Pearl. *Of Men and Women*. New York: John Day Company, 1941.

Montagu, Ashley. *The Natural Superiority of Women*. New York: Macmillan, 1953.

Reed, Ruth. *The Single Woman*. New York: The Macmillan Company, 1942.

Thoreau, Henry D. *Walden*. New York: The Heritage Press, 1939.

Periodicals

"American Woman's Dilemma." *Life*. Volume XXII (June 16, 1947). 101–111.

"For Men Only?" *Colliers*. Vol. CXXIV (November 12, 1949). 74.

Howitt, F. "Women Don't Give Women a Chance." *Good Housekeeping*. Vol. CXXIX (October, 1949). 33.

Lansing, E. "What More Do Women Want?" *Independent Woman*. Vol. XXXIX (April, 1952). 97.

"Women's Position in the World Today." *U. N. Bulletin*. Vol. IV (February 1, 1948). 94–96.

November 25, 1953
Suzy Hiatt
English XII

What I Want from a College Education

I do not know what I will get out of college. I know what I want to get out of it and what I do not want to get from my liberal arts education. What I want and what I get may very likely not be the same thing.

The first thing I want to receive from my education is a broad and general knowledge. I want to know what the world's great thinkers have thought, what her great statesmen have accomplished and what her great scientists have discovered. I do not want to be told who was right and who was wrong. I want to know the facts and judge for myself. Unfortunately however, I have a tendency to shy away from true knowledge. I tend to skim the surface and make snap decisions based on the few facts I feel I have mastered. No matter how much I learn later, these snap decisions tend to color the final assumption I make. This is a bad weakness, one that I must overcome if I am to get the true knowledge I want from my college education.

The second thing I want to learn in college is the value of a trained and organized mind. I want to learn to think and reason clearly and logically and to learn to use my mind during long and hard hours of study and thinking. I do not, however, want my mind to become a machine. An imagination is the most wonderful realm that was ever created and a mind mechanized beyond imagination must be a pretty dreary wasteland. But here again I have never worked my mind as hard as I should have, and I seriously doubt if I have the willpower to do so. Again, if I am to get anything from my college education I must change myself to do so.

The third objective of my college education will be meeting and dealing with new people. Nothing is so terrifying yet so broadening as having daily contact with a person who is deeply disturbed emotionally and learning how to cope with such a person and his problems. I do not only want to meet the nice, ordinary people like my high-school friends whom I will be seeing and corresponding with all my life, but the super-intellectuals who are slightly unbalanced, the "evil" girls who seem to have no sense of morals, the party-girls, and the kleptomaniacs.

But here again I am afraid of myself. I don't have the patience to deal with these people as well and sympathetically as I should. Pseudo-intellectuals annoy me more than any other type I can think of. Yet when I go to college I want to be patient and tolerant of them.

What I want out of college then, can only be achieved if I can correct the deficiencies in my own character. Perhaps the purpose of a college education is to correct these faults, but I believe any corrections must come from me. My ability to live with and correct these things will spell the difference for me between a broad, liberal-arts education and four wasted years.

Have Fun!

Homily Preached at St. John's Chapel, Episcopal Theological School, Cambridge, Massasachusetts (February 20, 1964)

In the Gospel for the Ember days, the gospel for our communion service yesterday and the service tomorrow, Jesus comes home to Nazareth and, as is his custom, goes to the synagogue. There he reads a lesson of his own choosing from the prophet Isaiah which our prayer book renders as follows:

> The Spirit of the Lord is upon me, because he hath anointed me to preach the gospel to the poor; he hath sent me to heal the broken-hearted, to preach deliverance to the captives, and recovering of sight to the blind, to set at liberty them that are bruised, to preach the acceptable year of the Lord.

An astounding text, full of difficult exegetical problems, one of the greatest passages of the greatest prophet—and the crowd in the synagogue waits eagerly to hear the promising young local boy expound on it. His opening sentence is a bombshell. "This day is the scripture fulfilled in your ears."

The people in the synagogue are slow to realize the full impact of what has been said. Like a parish hearing its own seminarian home on vacation they "all speak well of him" and congratulate themselves that one of their own reads so well. "Is this not Joseph's son?"

But as Jesus continues, the arrogance of his claim begins to dawn on them. The incident ends with people putting him out of the town, even attempting to throw him over a cliff. Jesus has offered them no signs and wonders to support his claim, he has merely stated with calm confidence the nature of his mission. The people are now offended by this young upstart, much as your home parish would be if you got up in the pulpit and announced your intention to make Christians of them.

Jesus often shocked people in the course of his ministry. We so often are told of his "great humility," yet time and again he made overwhelmingly arrogant claims like the one in this gospel. In fact it was for "blasphemy" such as this that he was ostensibly crucified. How can we read the Gospels and still sing "He came to us in lowliness of thought"?

I think our basic problem is a misunderstanding of humility. Even as we extol Jesus "meek and mild" we picture, I think, the self-effacing mousy people we occasionally notice on the periphery of our lives. We confuse humility with shyness, with insecurity, even with apparent vapidity.

True humility is a much stronger concept. In order to be humble a person must be secure in the knowledge that he possesses something of which he can be proud. If the humble man has nothing of which he can be proud, his humility is making a virtue of necessity. Humility is a virtue precisely because it is chosen—as Christ chose it.

There is an Appalachian Christmas carol that catches the full wonder and mystery of Christ's humility in his incarnation.

> If Jesus had wanted for any small thing
> A star in the sky, or a bird on the wing
> Or all of God's angels in heaven to sing
> Why he surely could've had it—for he was the king.

Jesus knew who he was—not perhaps in the sense that he could have straightened us out on his relationship to the divine Logos—but he did know that the Spirit of the Lord was upon him and he was anointed to preach the gospel to the poor. Secure in this knowledge he was free to accept all the abuse and humiliation he received at the hands of men. With our usual facility for error it was for his blasphemous pride that we killed him, not for his real offense—his humble obedience to his Father's will.

By his life, death and resurrection Jesus has showed us who he was. We see as his original hearers did not that his apparent arrogance was humble obedience. God chose him, in the words of our hymn, "to be a servant that we might be free." He was anointed to preach the gospel to the poor, and because we have heard that gospel and responded to it, we, and I mean by "we" all Christians, now have the same responsibility—we are anointed by the same spirit to the same task.

Our immediate reaction is that we can't do it. Preach the gospel to the poor when I can't even identify with their poverty? Heal the brokenhearted when their despair is as real to me as to them? Preach deliverance to the captives when my own anxieties hold me prisoner? Preach receiving of sight to the blind when they can't even see me waving to them? Set at liberty them that are bruised when I know that life offers nothing but bruising to many? And finally how can I preach the acceptable year of the Lord, the day of salvation, the time of which no man knows and which has been nearly 2000 years on the way?

We're right. We can't do it. Not as laymen, not as priests, not as bishops. We can't even be humble about our feeble attempts to do it for we have nothing to be proud of. Or have we?

I think we have. There is a saying I have seen on ancient tombstones—"Love is stronger than death." This, it seems to me, is a good summation of the gospel of Christ. When we look at the world to whom we are sent, we see only death where there should be life. God has chosen us, anointed us Christians with his Spirit. It is God's initiatory action, his love, that makes us free to preach this gospel and, through love, to conquer death itself. It is God's reconciliation of the world to himself in Christ that is, in fact, the gospel we are to preach. In our receiving of the gospel, our response to the grace of God is that we become "ministers of reconciliation." The Christian ministry is no more complex than that.

Yet in this place it seems far more complicated. We have three years here to ponder a call obeyed and to examine that call in all its ramifications. Right now I sense a general anxiety among my classmates about their impending ordinations. No one seems altogether clear on what one is ordained to do. There is a good deal of whistling in the dark, some proleptic mysticism, less joking about Whippel's, a little false humility and a general uneasiness among the seniors. Even those of us who won't be ordained suddenly discover that seminary, far from giving us answers and ground-rules for the "Christian Profession," a body of skills and knowledge, has given us instead a little fuller understanding of the Bible and new and deeper friends and enemies. Like the first century Christians when the end didn't come, we are nearly through seminary and still seeing through a glass darkly. We see in ourselves the signs of death—not bloody martyrdom, but the death of a life spent trying to keep the machinery going.

I suggest that our realization of this fact is possibly the best thing seminary education has given us. Hopefully in the process of our education here we, through our morbid introspection, clinical training experience, and the well-intentioned pastoral ministrations of our friends come to an increased self-awareness. We know our tendencies to death and are frightened by them.

But self-awareness is not self-acceptance, though it is a necessary forerunner for it. My experience in social work and in teaching leads me to believe that self-contempt rather than pride is perhaps man's besetting sin. Any thinking man is inevitably contemptuous of himself, for all of us fall short of our ambitions and our capacities.

The Gospel tells us however that God accepts us anyway. This is the freedom the Gospel promises—the conquering freedom of God's love. God accepts us for who we are—not always approving but demonstrably in his Son loving us at our most unlovable.

For seminarians this seems especially difficult to remember. God accepts you as whoever you are. He is not trying to make you another Jesus Christ, though he wants you to be free as Christ was free. He brought you to wherever you are right now. Give him a chance to work through and with you—a unique person, not "a seminarian," "a priest to be," "a minister's wife," or any other sort of role-filler. If God accepts us and uses us why do we find it so difficult to accept and use ourselves?

If we can relax and give back to God the prerogative to use us as He sees fit we will be free to preach the gospel. And we will be free to do it in full knowledge of our inability to do it, but confident, by the grace of God, that we are called to do it.

In conclusion, I would like to tell you a story about a child who began to be free to be himself by the grace of God. Jim, about eight years of age, lived in a well-regimented home where everything was done on schedule and with the greatest possible sense of purpose. School was followed by playtime, playtime by homework, homework by supper, supper by bathtime and finally the day closed with prayertime.

One evening Jim's mother was supervising his prayers at the appointed time. After hearing his "Now I lay me down to sleep" and intercessions for the family she said, "All right, Jim—now I want you to kneel quietly and listen to what God has to say to you."

For a minute or so Jim knelt dutifully. Suddenly he got up, went over to his toys and began to play. His mother said sternly, "Jim, I thought I told you to listen for God to speak to you."

"He did, Mother," Jim answered simply.

"He did? Well, what did he say?"

The little boy looked in triumph at his mother. "He said, 'Have fun, Jim.'"

God tells us to have fun too if we really listen to Him. He asks us to affirm our lives and ourselves in his service, not to fit into a mold he or anyone else has built and labelled "Christian." Jesus knew who he was and whose he was and was thereby free to preach the good news to the poor and miserable. Through his freedom we too are made free, not to act as pale imitations of him, but to be the person God has created each of us to be, and to suffer and rejoice in the world for which he died. Love such as this is indeed stronger than death.

Let us pray: Oh heavenly father, thou understandest all thy children; through thy gift of faith we bring our perplexities to the light of thy wisdom, and receive the blessed encouragement of thy sympathy, and a clearer knowledge of thy will. Glory be to thee for all thy gracious gifts, most especially the gift of thy son, our lord, Jesus Christ. Amen.

Notes: Why We Didn't Wait
for Ordination

Appended to "Fear of the Holy Spirit: Women's Ordination,"
Sermon at Christ Church, Oberlin, Ohio
(September 22, 1974)

want deal w. issue itself
    1) has been studied since 1919
    2) settled in the affirmative throughout Anglican Communion
    3) issue increasingly has been when + how
        So far only Hong Kong had taken step

why did we do it when + how we did
    1) 1964 statement—H of B—
        to exhaust every alternative way
        we feel we did that
        a) 2 gen'l conventions
        b) each of us had taken process as far as we could in
            diocese
        c) tried to find diocesan bps—always reasons why they
            couldn't
    2) But why not wait—only 2 more years
        a) delay = denial—very obvious in this case
        b) some had waited 60 years—I'd waited 10
            resistance hardening
        c) women's sit in world—good women leaving church
            missionary strategy

d) situation w. women in seminaries—
  needed positive action
e) Rosa Parks—"I'm tired"
So what next?
  1) can't accept invalidity either theo or personally
Oct 27 event at Riverside Church
  2) defense + action fund
  3) let bps know we're not alone + are
[Church like white African nations]

PART THREE

"BISHOP TO THE WOMEN"

Introduction to Part Three
"Bishop to the Women"

These representative selections of Sue Hiatt's written work span the periods immediately prior to and following the Philadelphia Ordination as well as the next decade as the numbers of women priests increased—along with the challenges they faced. Over about two decades, and prior to the election in September 1988 of the first woman Episcopal bishop, Barbara Harris, in Massachusetts, Sue became known across the nation and in other parts of the world as "bishop to the women," an informal term of respect and endearment that sprang up among women priests, deacons, seminarians, and laywomen who turned to her for counsel and encouragement (see Barbara Harris, "In Honor of an Unofficial Bishop," in the section called "Remembering Sue").

The first essay here is Hiatt's angry, ironic response to the national church's 1970 triennial convention, which had rejected the ordination of women priests. "Many of us will not be back. . . . We have other things to do. . . . I am sorry for the church that we will not be missed," she writes. Quoting a laywoman deputy to the convention, Hiatt quips, "No one need ever *say* certain people are less valued than others as long as the structure *acts* on that premise." A year later, in *Focus* magazine, she warns women of the three "major dangers to the hope of Christian women's emerging maturity": the weight of inertia, feelings of inferiority, and scattered rather than unified efforts to change the structures. During these years immediately preceding the Philadelphia Ordination, Sue Hiatt acknowledges that "sisterhood is a long time coming"—and that it our only hope.

In the weeks following the Philadelphia Ordination, Hiatt preached two sermons on the Holy Spirit. To ground the movement and her own role in it, she cites here, as she does so often throughout her ministry, the prophetic calls of Jesus and Isaiah to bring good news to the poor, release to captives, and freedom for the oppressed.

Admitting that for anyone "to claim the power of the Spirit is dangerous and arrogant," Hiatt suggests that "the only way to test the presence of the Spirit is by what happens when that presence is claimed." In both of these homilies, she does just that. She tells us what is happening in the aftermath of the Philadelphia Ordination. At Christ Church in Oberlin, Ohio, which has welcomed several women priests as its Eucharistic ministers over the objection of the bishop of Ohio, Hiatt lists various punitive reactions of bishops against the women priests and those, like the Rector Peter Beebe and people of Christ Church, who stand in solidarity with them. At Connecticut College in New London, she lifts up a number of positive signs that what is happening is very good: "Men are saying that they never realized how deeply they resisted women's self-affirmation or how much women's lack of choice restricted their own choice. Women, both in and out of the church, are beginning to realize that the gospel may have something to say to them about their lives and their ministries."

The sermon in Connecticut College's Harkness Chapel represents Sue Hiatt in one of her most enthusiastic preaching and teaching modes. In it she is upbeat and energetic, yet measured as ever by a humility which the reader of this volume can trace to her youth. There is nothing self-effacing about Sue Hiatt, and nothing apologetic, but rather she has a clarity—indeed, a certainty—that "the Spirit is leading" not only her, but *us*. She is not alone, but rather grounded with her sisters in the Holy Spirit. Quoting Martin Luther, she concludes: "Here we stand, we can do no other."

The essay "Why I Believe I Am Called to the Priesthood" places her own call, as one woman seeking to respond to God, in the context of the larger community of women who share this vocation. This is essential reading for anyone who wonders what it means "to be called" to anything, in this case to a particular ministry that is barred to women on the basis of long-standing prejudice that issues from the patriarchal fear of women's sacred power.

Shortly after the Philadelphia Ordination, Sue Hiatt and I were invited to join the faculty of the Episcopal Divinity School in Cambridge, Massachusetts, an invitation heralding the seminary's alliance with the new women priests as well as the ongoing movement for women's ordination. In March 1975, Hiatt preached in the EDS chapel on the tenth anniversary of the murder in Alabama of Jonathan Daniels, one of her seminary friends. Daniels had been shot down by a white man who was aiming to kill Ruby Sales, a young African-American woman who, decades later, would be a student at the Episcopal Divinity School where Sue was on the faculty. Jonathan Daniels had stepped into the line of fire and, as the news of his slaying spread, the young seminarian had been raised up as a martyr and had become one of the Episcopal Divinity School's most esteemed alums. Jonathan Daniels and Judith Upham, another seminarian, were among thousands of Americans who had gone to Selma to join the march for freedom in the spring of 1965.

In this commemorative sermon, Sue Hiatt quotes Judy Upham: "We had serious questions about the probability of any action being effective, but the issue seemed to be not effectiveness, but faithfulness." This strong current—faithfulness—runs through Hiatt's own ministry. Linking herself to Jon and Judy's "reasons" for having done what they did ten years earlier, she says, "A Christian's reasons for the hope that is in us can be simply and succinctly stated in three short sentences: Christ has died. Christ is risen. Christ will come again." These "three short sentences" undergirded the faith—and as such, the prophetic leadership and priestly presence—of Sue Hiatt.

Because Sue Hiatt was not especially interested in theology as an academic discipline, she seldom bothered to explain how she understood such traditional theological affirmations as "Christ has died. Christ is risen. Christ will come again." She knew what she meant and she assumed (rightly, I believe) that her understanding was in keeping with the traditions of the Episcopal Church. Simply put, Sue Hiatt was affirming the reality of Jesus's ongoing (risen) spirit working in our lives, and her belief that this spirit (Christ) would "come again" more fully—perhaps in this world, and most surely in the eternal realm of God, what some people call "heaven" or "eternity." Trying to explain this kind of theological affirmation was not something Sue Hiatt would customarily have done. The reason I am doing it in this introductory piece is to help the reader realize the relatively traditional Christian foundations of Hiatt's radically prophetic faith.

The next two pieces presage a theme that grows in Hiatt's public work and private reflections throughout her life: the fear that women priests, once ordained, would make peace with the ongoing oppression of women and others who had been marginalized by mainline Christian churches in the United States and elsewhere. Sue Hiatt deeply desired that women continue working together to transform the church at its core into a more justice-making, prophetic community. In "The Challenge of the Churches: Why Bother?" (addressed to an audience at Radcliffe College, her alma mater), she asks why women should even bother with seeking to be ordained. She gives a couple of good reasons but follows with the warning: "If we allow ourselves to become part of the system as it is, we will simply compound the oppression of women." Two years later, in her sermon at the 1979 ordination of her friend Sandra Hughes Boyd, Hiatt recounts the scene from George Orwell's *Animal Farm* where the revolutionary animals become "so thoroughly acclimated to human ways that they cannot be distinguished from the men." "I fear a day," preaches our bishop to the women, "when we will no longer be able to tell the women clergy from the men."

"Women in the Episcopal Diaconate and Priesthood" is a speech Hiatt made at a women's history conference ten years after the Philadelphia Ordination. Here she reflects on women's recent history in the Episcopal Church, including the significance of the order of "deaconess" which had long been marginalized within the church and which had not been given much recognition by the movement for women's ordination to the priesthood. This presentation by Hiatt is a fine historical piece, in which she makes the critical connection between women priests and those deaconesses and other women on whose lives we women priests have built our own.

Sue Hiatt considered "Fair Harvard's Daughters," published in the journal of her alma mater, Radcliffe College, in 1985, to be among her best written pieces. Not one to boast, Sue told me repeatedly how glad she was the *Radcliffe Quarterly* had published this essay and how glad she was to have written it. In this piece, she raises again the *Animal Farm* scenario in which the pigs begin imitating the men with whom they have struggled for their own liberation. This brief essay is one of Sue Hiatt's finest in both its literary flair and its ethical punch.

Part three concludes with "The Great Thing About Mary," published in *The Witness* in 1986. Not surprisingly, in this call for the election and consecration of women bishops, Hiatt contends that "the great thing about Mary" was not her son but that "she heard the word of God and kept it."

C.H.

The Week That Was

Response to the Episcopal General Convention's Refusal to Authorize the Ordination of Women Priests

ISSUES, Monday, October 19, 1970
(Paper issued daily during General Convention of
Episcopal Church, Houston, Texas, Oct. 1970)

Saturday morning a majority of the House of Deputies voted in favor of a resolution endorsing the right of women to seek ordination to the priesthood and consecration to the Episcopate. The resolution was defeated. As one of the women affected most immediately by this action I offer some random reflections.

Throughout this week I have been erroneously described by the press as a young seminarian. I am neither. I graduated from seminary six years ago. One of my male seminary colleagues is a bishop—most are rectors, many are delegates to this convention. Many of my female seminary colleagues have left the church, few serve professionally in it on any level. I hold a responsible professional position in my diocese. The priest with whom I share this ministry—a contemporary both chronologically and educationally—is called many things in the local press, but never to my recollection "an attractive young man" or "a recent seminary graduate." When he is quoted publicly details of his marital status or family life are not added for "human interest."

The hopeful note about this week has been the support and encouragement of the women at this convention. Old ladies, young girls, deaconesses, nuns, seminarians, housewives, professional women all have demonstrated that they affirm women's freedom to be persons. I am gratified that attempts to make women postulants look ridiculous were met not with nervous laughter but with stony silence. Efforts to flatter and cajole women on the basis of their "superiority" (the pedestal approach) were equally ineffective.

A Black brother, knowing so well what was coming, made a point of sitting with me during Saturday morning's "debate" in the House of Deputies. I heard myself described as a threat to the entire ecumenical movement, the reef on which fifty years of negotiations would suddenly be wrecked. I was described as a creature inherently incapable of prophecy (Jon Daniels once thanked me for speaking to him in a prophetic voice), whose highest glory was to emulate Christ's mother. Just how I might do this or why I should want to was not explained. The church is not ready for me, therefore I should wait a decade or two (after all, young seminarians should practice the virtue of patience). Some of the speakers said that some of their best friends were women who to the best of their knowledge were content in their place. During this dismal recital someone asked me how I felt. I referred him to the brother beside me who has much longer experience than I with what I was feeling. He had nothing to say.

Not many middle-aged white Americans have the opportunity to experience the receiving end of the racist mentality. It hurts and one must take it personally because in the end it is intended personally—as an attack on one's personhood. As Dr. Barbara Williams said so incisively on Friday, no one need ever *say* certain people are less valued than others as long as the structure *acts* on that premise. Many of us will not be back in Jacksonville. We have other things to do in the name of Christ outside the church that are probably more important and certainly more productive. I am sorry for the church that we will not be missed.

The Female Majority
Can Sisterhood Survive?

Focus, November 1971, 1–2

Anyone who is not aware that "the woman problem" is big in the churches this year would not have bothered to pick up this issue of FOCUS at all. Therefore, we can begin by assuming that the reader knows that all is not well in the church kitchens, parlors, Sunday School rooms and sacristies of America.

Women in churches throughout the world but especially in America are beginning to realize that while the bulk of "maintenance" work in the churches is done by women, authority and decision-making in those same churches is exclusively a male prerogative. The majority of the world's Christians are women, but with a very few rule-proving exceptions, the churches' leaders are male.

This realization is taking many forms. In churches where women are "de jure" excluded from decision-making roles (e.g., Roman Catholic, Episcopal), they are beginning to unite behind efforts to change repressive canon law and tradition. The Episcopal Church has recently acknowledged women to be within the diaconate, the first of that church's three holy orders. In the Roman Catholic Church, a Canadian Cardinal has even spoken right out loud in Rome at the current synod of bishops of the possibility of women priests. In those churches where the exclusion of women is "de facto" (e.g., Presbyterian, United Church of Christ), women are beginning to question the subtle ways in which they are kept in their place. Both the Presbyterian Church, USA and the UCC have recently set up task forces on women at the highest levels of church polity and are promoting educational materials for study on the local level. The emerging self-consciousness of women in the churches is of course part of a larger movement: a diverse groping of women toward new identities, often lumped by the media under the amorphous and vaguely threatening title "women's liberation." Churchwomen seem to have an unholy fear of that label, possibly because our mildest attempts to re-define our roles (e.g., refusing to serve as secretary simply because we're the only woman on the committee) are interpreted by churchmen as part of a "woman libber's" plot. Yet churchwomen often are motivated by the women's liberation talk that is in the air to look more closely at our assigned roles in church and to find in them exactly the stereotyping and patronizing attitudes the liberationists are talking about. On the other hand, churchwomen have been led to join the women's liberation movement as a result of the treatment we receive when we attempt to participate in the life of the church as fully competent adults—and are rebuffed.

The fact that women are realizing that the churches do not treat us as full partners in the spreading of the kingdom is a hopeful sign. The seeds of full humanity for women are in the Gospels, but they are only now beginning to germinate. This is a crucial moment in American churches regarding the issue of female participation. Perhaps the last great hope for them rests in the course they take in dealing with it.

At this critical moment there seem to me to be three major dangers to the hope of Christian women's emerging maturity. They are as follows:

I. WEIGHT OF INERTIA

In institutions as in physics, inertia is a powerful force. It will take a sustained, concerted effort—no doubt to the point of causing dissention and unpleasantness—for women to break out of our traditional stereotypes in significant numbers. Recently, a body of men, clergy and lay, in my own diocese objected to a plan to reserve twelve seats on diocese council because they felt twelve women could not be found among our communicants who would be competent and willing to serve. The tradition of female inferiority runs so deeply in all of us, and especially among the clergy, that it can be overcome only by a long and steadfast effort.

Those of us interested in making this effort must concentrate on three fronts. First, we must insure that teachers of pastoral theology and seminary students in their charge are exposed to new pastoral models for dealing with women. A woman beginning to question old roles and values is more often than not stopped dead in her tracks on this quest if she goes to her pastor for help. Most clergy are badly prepared to counsel women—first, because there were so few women in their seminary classes and secondly, because they often see the church's role as defender of the home and family. The best way to defend these institutions is to keep women relying on them for "fulfillment." Despite the evidence that Christ was itinerant and unwed, American churches have set up the two-parent nuclear family as the ideal "Christian" arrangement, to the grief and loneliness of the single, the elderly and the divorced who also profess the Christian faith. Woman's changing consciousness poses a threat to this arrangement that many pastors cannot deal with objectively. Seminary is the place to insist that our clergy start re-examining what they really believe and how it affects their counseling.

Next we must identify and encourage those people in the churches who are experimenting with new models of leadership for women. We should applaud and publicize experimental and unusual ministries of women in denominational magazines and elsewhere. We should encourage women who are serving in unusual roles to speak about their work to church groups, especially women's groups.

Finally, we must constantly provide support and counsel for those women challenging tradition. I am tired of reminding my bishop that he should no longer address the clergy as "my brothers" now that we have women clergy. Although fiercely supportive of women in the ministry, he does it solely from force of habit. If I could call upon others to remind him occasionally, I would feel better and his habit would change more quickly. Allies are crucial for anyone struggling to combat inertia, especially allies who know how to work effectively in the political structures of the churches and are willing to pass along that skill and knowledge.

II. FEELING INFERIOR

For centuries the churches have warned against the sin of pride. In the court of King David as in the courts of medieval kings and princes it was often only the prophet or confessor who put any kind of check on the will of a rapacious ruler. Pride has more commonly been considered a masculine sin, but in our time it has been the women who have heard the stern warnings of Nathan and St. Paul. As a result, Christian women have become unhealthily subservient, even masochistic, in the name of humility and self-sacrifice. Women must gain confidence in themselves as people before they will be able to provide the kind of leadership and judgment so badly needed to change the church and the world.

The only way women can gain this confidence is through accomplishment and the feelings of success. Unfortunately women tend to belittle our successes rather than admit to competence, so steeped are we in the cultural stereotypic image that "women can't do anything right." The "consciousness-raising" aspects of women's liberation can be very helpful in moving women to identify our low self-esteem and its roots. This process can be adapted for any group of women, and modified to fit the needs of the particular group. Study guides are available for churchwomen's groups specifically to help them discover who and where they are. I recommend the Rev. Letty Russell's *Women's Liberation in a Biblical Perspective,* a six-session study guide prepared jointly by the United Presbyterian Women and the YWCA as a good place for a group of women to begin. (Note: order from The National Board, YWCA, Bureau of Communications, Room 605, Lexington Avenue, New York 10022, $.50 each and group discount.)

III. SCATTERED EFFORTS

Many churchwomen are engaged in the effort to gain a fuller place for women in church life, but most of us are virtually alone and isolated from women with similar interests. Women are often suspicious due to a long and deeply internalized tradition of female rivalry. Many professional women have made their way by shutting off the world of women. We are reluctant to make common cause with other women for fear we will be stereotyped and lose our "special place" in the world of men. Laywomen find little support among women on the parish level and find it difficult to identify other women who feel as they do and willing to work for change. Many women, especially young women, who have recognized church patronization have long departed to use their talents elsewhere.

Even when women do get together we are easily diverted from examining our own situation. This is done by pointing to much more obvious and flagrant oppressions (i.e., race and war) and suggesting that women are spoiled and self-serving not to devote all of our energies to "more pressing" battles. It is also done by pointing out that men, too, are oppressed and, we can't change that without changing the whole society, so it's useless to begin. These arguments are readily accepted by women (especially churchwomen who get very nervous about "selfish" concerns) as a welcome relief from dealing with the deep ramifications of our oppression as women.

Mary Daly has called women's mutual distrust of each other "horizontal violence." She adds that violence against each other rather than the oppressor is a characteristic of any oppressed group. She argues strongly that women must develop a sense of "sisterhood," mutual trust and support among ourselves as strong as our individual bonds with individual men which have sustained us in the past. Sisterhood is based on self-esteem for we cannot respect other women until we respect ourselves.

Sisterhood is a Long Time Coming. It begins by identifying those women and groups of women within and across denominational and geographic lines who share our belief in women and our potential to transform the church. We are beginning to establish a network of churchwomen with similar goals through such means as newsletters and personal contacts. I know of ecumenical groups of women working on the problems of women in churches in Boston, New York, Northampton, Mass., Philadelphia and Atlanta, Georgia. There are also groups within denominations, women's caucuses in dioceses, synods, seminaries and at every level of church life.

Such groups can have powerful effects on the churches if they are and will get in touch with each other. For example, if an ecumenical group were to call on an Episcopal bishop in a particular location who refused to ordain women, they just might persuade him to reconsider. Or if a local caucus of UCC women were to see a Synod executive about the lack of opportunity for women in the Synod, his consciousness about women would almost certainly be altered.

Sisterhood is powerful—but it is slow in development and subject to harassment both subtle and overt. It will need to be strong to survive the backlash of "happy women are well-adjusted to domesticity" that will inevitably follow the current women's liberation ferment. Yet it is the cornerstone of any kind of sustained change in the commitment of the majority of Christians—*the female majority.*

Fear of the Holy Spirit
Women's Ordination

Sermon Preached at Christ Church, Oberlin, Ohio
(September 22, 1974)

In the name of God; Creator, redeemer, Sanctifier. Amen.
glad to be in Oberlin—my great aunts—1st women educ in my
family Oberlin grads
I don't often preach about women for a feast of the Holy Spirit
will today
start w a few remarks about Holy Spirit
A) often thought of as 3ʳᵈ (+ last) person of the [trinity]
much neglected in theological circles—eg I noticed in cor-
respondence between bp + woman priest much reference to
judgment of God the Father, mercy of God the Son—but no
mention of prodding of God the Holy Spirit
B) I think the reason is that Holy Spirit is most frightening person
of [trinity] to churchmen and theologians because she is
dynamic and unpredictable—
1) Listen to what she sends Isaiah to do:
"to bring good tidings to the afflicted
to bind up the broken hearted
to proclaim liberty to the captives and the opening
of the prison to those who are bound
to proclaim the year of the Lord's favor
and the day of vengeance of our God"

2) Such activity is dangerous, radical and of course threatening to anyone in a position of power—bishops no less than kings—

3) Such activity is also arrogant—making mere humans such as Isaiah the intermediaries bidden to do the work of God himself. You may remember that Jesus was driven from the synagogue in his home town and nearly [text illegible] passage from Isaiah and announcing that the same Spirit of the Lord was upon him to fulfill those same tasks.

C) Religious people have a difficult time with the Holy Spirit precisely because we prefer to worship a God who is under control, whose ways are known and who can be trusted to feel as we do about events

D) But we just get God under control—housed in a particular kind of building, worshipped in a particular kind of ritual with a certain type of music and language considered "appropriate" to holy occasions—when bang—God the Holy Spirit is prodding us again continually showing us that our notion of God has been too small—Little wonder we resist the action of God the Holy Spirit for she continually brings our notion of who God is up short

II And so it was on July 29th, the feast of Mary and Martha when four Bishops participated in an irregular ordination of eleven women priests in obedience to the leading of this same demanding, arrogant and unpredictable Spirit—

A) And the Church's reaction, sadly, has been close to that of the faithful Jews who strove to rid their synagogue of the blasphemous Jesus. As one commentator has remarked "That these women should choose to add to Martha's traditional roles of adorning the altar...caring for the children, and ironing vestments that of Mary, the inspired listener, has apparently rocked the Church as no recent wars, famines or more usual injustices have done. . . ."

1) The House of bishops reacted swiftly by declaring "the necessary conditions" for validity lacking on July 29th. If that language confuses you, you are getting an accurate reading

of that emergency House of Bishops meeting—confusion and panic seemed to permeate their deliberations. In spirit of commentator above, amazing how the women's issue could get H of B together as racism, Vietnam, Nixon never did.

2) Presentments for ecclesiastical trial have been filed against at least two of the women, the four bishops, and approximately 12 priests who participated in the laying on of hands.

3) Bishops in the jurisdictions have prohibited all eleven women and some of the ordaining bishops from exercising any of their priestly functions.

4) Charges are hurled about breaking canons, collegiality, catholic tradition. We 15 are accused of dividing the Church, making the church look foolish, intending to "get" various imagined enemies and even of plotting to destroy the church—

A murderous spirit of revenge and retribution has been unleashed in Zion—and there is no peace.

B) Was this our intention? Certainly not. Had we known what the reaction would be would we have proceeded? Certainly—

For we proceeded in obedience to the leading of the Spirit and we have confidence that ultimately that is what God requires of us

We regret the pain and division the church is experiencing. However we know that this is precisely how the Holy Spirit works in and through us—

1) The past-oriented among us—those who are comfortable with a static God and who see the Church as a refuge from the world need to be challenged—

2) The future-oriented among us—those who constantly expect God to lead them in new and unexpected directions and who see the church as affirming God's action in the world also need to be challenged—challenged to reveal the work of the Spirit to our brothers and sisters in Zion

C) Our present divisiveness is hard and cruel for all of us—Many were hurt + stunned by the ordination itself. Many others, women and men, are being hurt and stunned by the church's swift and brutal reaction to that ordination—These people—many of you here—are mourning in Zion at the apparent triumph of law over Gospel

III So what can I say to you? Have I helped hasten the church's apparent suicide by forcing the issue on women in priesthood? Should I apologize and leave you to patch things up with those who feel we are wrong? Possibly but I cannot do that at this time. I am confident we were not wrong and the Holy Spirit is as much with us now in the aftermath as she was on July 29th

A) I am comforted + strengthened in this conviction by the lessons of Church history—

Time and again in Christian history it has looked like the Church was about to die. Time and again the church has grown fat and powerful and suffered the fate of the collapse of the particular nation or regime it has allowed itself to become identified with. The church we know is in such peril now—Over the past 200 years Christianity has become dangerously identified with Western imperialism and exploitation. The era of world dominance by the western powers is coming to a cataclysmic end, and the church is in danger of ending with it.

B) However, there is another strain in Christian history—The church has always escaped these cataclysms by virtue of small bands of Christians in out of the way places who survived the purges by virtue of being too powerless or too distant to pursue. The Church survived the fall of Rome in the 5th Century through small bands of monks and missionaries far away in France. It survived the collapse of the Frankish kingdom in the 10th century thru small bands of Christians far away in Ireland and Scotland. Always it survives because, quite peripherally to its main business, it had brought the Gospel to insignificant and remote people. In a very real way the stone that the builders reject often becomes the chief cornerstone

C) I used to think in viewing the approaching end of our society, that the church would continue in Asia or Africa where small bands of Christians would keep the faith alive through the dark ages to come. However recently I've begun to wonder if it might not survive among us—the disaffected Christians right here today who are trying to follow the lead of the Holy Spirit. That lead may take us out of the church we have known—it may lead us to deposition and excommunication but perhaps that, too, is part of God the Holy Spirit's plan. Perhaps this time the new Church will survive in the ruins of the old—perhaps the ordination on July 29th and the uproar stemming from it are a hopeful sign. That ordination may have been more timely than we can yet know—part of the Holy Spirit's plan to build continuity of the old church (women ordained by the laying on of hands) into a new beginning (a church in exile without a hierarchy and without formal organization). Only time will tell, but I am increasingly hopeful

IV And that hope—and an inner peace and certainty about my vocation is all I can offer to those of you who mourn in Zion.

Finally let us never forget the promise the Spirit has made to us

"to give us a garland instead of ashes
the oil of gladness instead of mourning
the mantle of praise instead of a faint spirit
that we may be called oaks of righteousness
the planting of the Lord, that he may be glorified"
Amen

The Life of the Spirit

Sermon Preached at Harkness Chapel, Connecticut College,
New London, Connecticut (November 24, 1974)
11:00 a.m.

Speaker: The Reverend Suzanne Hiatt
One of the women ordained to the Episcopal priesthood this past
summer in Philadelphia.

Scripture Lessons: Psalm 146, Isaiah 61:1–4, Luke 4:16–30

In the Name of God: Creator, Redeemer, Sanctifier. Amen.

In the lessons that Mr. Robb just read, both the prophet Isaiah in
the Old Testament and Jesus in the New Testament claim that they do
what they do because "the Spirit of the Lord is upon me." Today I'd like
to reflect with you on this Spirit—the sanctifier, the third person of the
Trinity. Who is the Spirit? What does She do and what does it mean to
claim that the Spirit of the Lord is upon me?

The first thing to be said is that to claim the power of the Spirit is
dangerous and arrogant. There is no way that such a claim is subject to
external, rational, objective verification. To claim the guidance of the
Holy Spirit is to behave rather like Flip Wilson's character Geraldine
who always seeks to excuse herself with a wide-eyed assertion that "the
devil made me do it!" There is a temptation for us to hide behind the
Spirit as mover when we can't otherwise account for why something
happens. The Spirit can be blamed for something good in the same magical way Geraldine blames the devil for something not so good.

And indeed there is a magical element about the Holy Spirit in both
the Old and the New Testaments. Throughout the Bible the imagery

of the Holy Spirit is both magical and powerful, and often destructive as well. The "Ruach" of God, the Spirit that moved on the waters at creation, is seen as a powerful wind. Often this Ruach is described as wind, not a gentle breeze, but a strong gale that can and does rearrange the landscape. In the New Testament, this same Spirit is often described in terms of fire, as when John describes the baptism of fire that the Messiah will bring, or when the Spirit descends on the believers at Pentecost in the form of tongues of fire. In all this imagery the Spirit of the Lord is experienced as a powerful, irresistible force that impinges on the lives of believers.

Because Her visitations result in unexpected and unpredictable turnings, "religious" people don't much like the Holy Spirit. She keeps messing up our plans and breaking our rules just when we thought we knew what God wanted of us. A recent example of this discomfiture with the Spirit in my own denomination, the Episcopal Church, came in the reaction of our bishops to the irregular ordination of eleven women priests on July 29th. In the ensuing verbiage there was very little appeal to God the Holy Spirit. God the Father, yes. He was often appealed to as judge and former of the order of creation. God the Son has also been invoked for His compassion and willingness to forgive those who break rules. But little mention has been made by the bishops of God in the person of the Holy Spirit. We "religious" people like our God under control. We want God to be predictable and appeasable. We want to know what the rules are so that we can follow them and be "all right" with God. But God in the person of the Holy Spirit will not be contained in the rules we've made for Him. We are uneasy about the new directions we might be pushed into by the leading of the Spirit.

So God the Spirit is dynamic and unpredictable. Most distressing, She is apt to break into our lives—to anoint us as Isaiah and Jesus put it—to ask us to do things and to go in directions we'd never have dreamed of. It is important that we be able to recognize the anointing of the Spirit and to distinguish it from other motivations we might have. How can we know when the Spirit of God is pushing us?

How do we test our calling?

We can begin by looking at ways in which the call of the Spirit cannot be verified. First, we cannot judge our call by how the works we claim in the name of God the Spirit are received by others. Jesus's experience demonstrated all too well that a prophet is indeed without honor in his own country. That what we do in the name of the Spirit is viewed as destructive of institutions is no more necessarily proof that our call is *not* of God than it is proof that it is. Nor can the presence of the Spirit be verified by what are traditionally called "the gifts of the Spirit"—such unusual occurrences as speaking in tongues, or prophesying, or going into a state of ecstatic trance. Very often Christians have viewed the manifestation of these "gifts" as the true test of the presence of the Spirit, and indeed such gifts are real and thrilling. But in themselves they are not worth very much. Being spirit-filled is not another form of "high," though often such feelings go with that state. To "feel" the presence of the Spirit is not in itself evidence of the Spirit's presence, as St. Paul warned the believers at Corinth. Such gifts are real, but Paul calls them "lesser gifts."

According to the Bible witness the only way to test the presence of the Spirit is by what happens when that presence is claimed. The Spirit comes to people with specific tasks that are to be done in the name of God and by his power. In today's lessons these things are spelled out in three places; in the psalm, in the prophet, and in the gospel we are told that the Spirit has anointed the chosen *to the end* that the blind may receive their sight, the poor may have the good news preached to them, the captives may be freed, the oppressed may receive justice. It is clear in reading the Bible that how much these things happen is the true test of the Spirit's presence. In fact, Jesus's answer to John the Baptist when he expresses some question about Jesus's messiahship is that the blind receive their sight and the captives and the oppressed are being freed. The proof that Jesus is "he that is to come" is in what is happening.

So that is the test that we must apply when we claim to be led by the Spirit. Do the blind receive their sight? Are the oppressed and the captives freed?

When eleven women were ordained to the priesthood in the Episcopal Church on July 29th we felt led by the Holy Spirit and we continue to make that claim. We had seen and felt the winds of liberation blowing among women, not in the church, but in the world. We felt that wind was of God, that the blind were receiving their sight and captives were being freed. Women were affirming their wholeness as persons and we saw this as the Spirit's work. By the way, the Spirit of God often works in the world when the church won't admit Her. Time and again in the history of our God and His people forces break in from outside to call us back to what we should be doing. We believe that this is such a time. We want to bring this message of freedom for women into the church and have her own and embrace it.

And we are still working to that end. We still claim the anointing of the Spirit of the Lord as surely as did Isaiah and Jesus. We claim it to the same ends—the spreading of the Good News of the kingdom of God. The claim is as arrogant and as irrational as it ever was. Our reception among our own has been about the same, too.

But none of that is important. We continue to ask ourselves, do the blind receive their sight? Are the poor being preached to? Are the oppressed being freed?

We see signs that all these things are happening. Men are saying that they never realized how deeply they resisted women's self-affirmation or how much women's lack of choice restricted their own choice. Women, both in and out of the church, are beginning to feel that the Gospel may have something to say to them about their lives and their ministries. Blacks, women and laymen are saying "no" to the quiet passive role the church has assigned them in the past. They are seeing that God is calling them to His work in the world, not to be safe and secure in a church that shuts out storms and controversy.

These are small signs that the Spirit was indeed present on July 29th and in its aftermath. We continue to preach in the light of these signs that "now is the acceptable time of the Lord." We preach with fear and trembling, for our claim is arrogant and the pain of many of our brothers and sisters in hearing our message is real and distressing. But we also preach with love and joy, for we are sure the Spirit is still leading us.

What may happen next is out of our control. We may all be deposed or the church may accept our priesthood. But whatever the outcome, we can only say like Martin Luther before us,

"Here we stand, we can do no other."

Amen.

Why I Believe I Am Called
to the Priesthood

"Why I Believe I Am Called to the Priesthood."
In *The Ordination of Women Pro and Con*, edited by
Michael P. Hamilton and Nancy S. Montgomery, 30–42.
New York: Morehouse Barlow Co., 1975

There is an old joke seminarians tell—it was told to me many years ago when I was in seminary. It concerns an elderly Christian who was asked by a minister, who was trying to ascertain his parishioner's theological views, whether he believed in infant baptism. The old man's response left no doubt as to where he stood. "Believe in it?" he replied, "Hell, I've *seen* it!"

I have seen the ordination of women to the priesthood. Furthermore, I have experienced in my own life God's call to women to be priests. Not only did I myself struggle to understand the nature of that call for many years, but in my ministry to women during the past three years I have met and talked with hundreds of Episcopal women also in the midst of trying to decipher what God wants of them. As this is written, there are approximately one hundred and fifty women deacons serving in the Episcopal Church, most of whom are clear that their call is to priesthood. There is probably a further hundred in the process of seeking ordination through diocesan structures. In the spring of 1974, fifteen percent of the students in Episcopal seminaries were women. The proportion is no doubt higher now, for the number of women in Episcopal seminaries doubled every year from the fall of 1971 through the fall of 1974. In addition, as I travel around the church, I am often approached, usually shyly and with embarrassment, by women who confide to me that they feel called to ordained ministry and are seeking advice on how best to test that call.

The first question these astonishing statistics lead us to ask is, "Why now?" Why, in the seventh decade of the twentieth century after Christ, is God suddenly doing something new and strange in the calling of women to priesthood? Even if we allow that it is actually part of a movement that began in the nineteenth century, God's call to women may still strike us as suspiciously sudden in the sweep of Christian history.

Perhaps, as often happens, the sudden change is not in God's action but in our ability to perceive and recognize that action. Women have been called to priesthood for a long time—but the Church's utter inability to recognize that call and women's own deep diffidence about such a shocking vocation have kept it hidden. There is evidence, still sketchy and dim, that women have had priestly, and even episcopal ministries in Christian history, but, apart from the important role which abbesses played, until recently sainthood has been the only ecclesiastical role open to both women and men. In the past, women who felt called to priesthood hardly dared admit such a call to themselves. Those for whom such a call may have been irresistible, and who dared share it, were no doubt told that it was impossible because God does not call women to priesthood and, therefore, they had better re-examine their spiritual state and purge their souls of such dangerous delusions. In fact, one woman was told almost exactly that by her bishop in 1972.

The church's slowness to recognize God's work is not new nor is it unusual. In the third chapter of the first book of Samuel in the Old Testament there is a poignant illustration of this deeply human tendency. The child Samuel, apprenticed to the elderly priest Eli, awakens in the night to the sound of a voice calling his name. Thinking that Eli is calling, he awakens the old man to do his bidding. Eli sends him back to bed since he did not call. Again Samuel hears the call and again he awakens Eli who sends him back to bed (somewhat testily we might guess). When Samuel awakens Eli a third time asking if he called it finally occurs to the old man that the call may be from the Lord and he tells Samuel to respond. When the Lord calls again it is with a message of destruction for Eli so terrible that the boy does not dare to tell the old man. Eli insists, however, and when Samuel relays the message his response is "It is the Lord; let him do what seems good to him." Belatedly Eli recognizes the work of the Lord and his obligation to accede to it.

Women have heard that voice calling in the night. Some of the less timid have gently nudged the sleeping church and asked her if she called. Somewhat testily, the church has replied that she did not. Many women have taken "no" for an answer and gone about the Lord's work in other ways. Others, however, have heard the voice again and have asked the church a second time if she called. Still she answers that she did not, but the voice persists and the realization that it is God and perhaps not (yet) the church that is calling grows stronger. Women who have been called are giving up that conviction less readily and nudging the church yet a third time. Her response is yet to be determined.

If one starts to speak of voices in the night, one takes on an obligation to try to explain just what one means. What is the nature of God's call to priesthood? Can we women be somewhat more articulate and concrete about the nature and form of "our call"? Such an assignment is difficult, but like most difficult tasks no doubt good for the soul. Women who claim a call to priesthood find themselves quizzed about the matter endlessly; I suspect that is why so many women are terribly embarrassed about it. They trust the call, but dread the ordeal of attempting to "justify" it to their fellow Christians for the rest of their lives.

Women who claim a call to priesthood report a tremendous variety of ways in which they experience that call. Some say they have known since girlhood that they were called to priesthood. One woman priest, now eighty years old, tells the story of confronting her mother with her vocation. When she was eleven years old, her mother came into her room one evening for what she now realizes was scheduled to be a little chat about the birds and the bees. The mother began by asking her daughter what she wanted to be when she grew up, fully expecting the standard response that she wanted to be a mother and planning to lead from that response into the particulars of motherhood. When the daughter responded instead that she wanted to be a priest, the mother fled from the room in tears. The daughter recalls the episode as the only time she ever saw her Victorian mother either run or cry. Later, in 1914 when she entered college she told the college president that she wanted to enter The General Theological Seminary when she was graduated. Together they planned a course of study that would prepare her for seminary since the college president was certain that the priesthood would be open to women by 1918. She finally went to The General Theological Seminary in 1972.

Others come to their vocations later in life. One woman, an architect by training and profession, became interested and active in the church when her children were small and the family was living in a small town. She discovered that she was a natural pastor to other women and decided she needed some training to deal with the problems that were being brought to her. At the same time, she realized that her interest in others and her ability to help grew out of her Christian commitment. When her children entered school she began part-time seminary work and is now in the ordination process.

The women called to priesthood are a varied lot. Some are "cradle" Episcopalians, others are new to the Episcopal church and some are new to the Christian faith. Some are Anglo-Catholics, others are evangelicals, many are somewhere in between. They are liberal and conservative, feminists and antifeminists. They are mothers, and grandmothers, and great-grandmothers. Some are single, some are married, some are widowed, some are divorced. Some are young, some are old, most are in-between. They are debutantes and blue-collar wives. Most are white and middle-class, but some are Black, or Hispanic; others are poor or rich. Some are pursuing full-time ministry; others plan part-time jobs or "worker priest" vocations. Some are daughters, wives or widows of bishops and priests, others have parents or husbands who wouldn't know what a bishop was. All want to test their call in accordance with the guidelines the church imposes and many are in the process of doing so. Some will decide they are not called to priesthood, others will be told by the church that they do not meet the standards. All will be asked repeatedly to explain and elaborate on their motivations.

In short, the women called to priesthood are very much like the men who are called to priesthood. There is one difference and that is that the women's announcement that they feel called will be greeted with a good deal more skepticism and dismay than will their brothers'. Men who feel called to priesthood are not generally required to apologize for that fact nor to justify their reasons for not wishing to remain in the laity in the same way women are. In fact a devoted Christian layman will often experience pressure from other Christians to be ordained priest so he "can serve the Lord full time."

It is good to remember that the basic call that all Christians share is to witness to the Lord Jesus Christ in the world. There have been times—and such times will come again—when all Christians must be ready to stand by that call to the death. In the first epistle of Peter, Christians are advised to "Always be prepared to make a defense to anyone who calls you to account for the hope that is in you, yet do it with gentleness and reverence. . . ." Nowadays nobody asks the average Christian to make that defense in the normal course of events. Clergy are asked more often than laypeople and women clergy more often than men.

And so finally I am being asked to account for the hope that is in me. I have spoken of voices in the night and promised a fuller explanation. I will not engage in yet another theological treatise on priesthood and what that may or may not mean in the twentieth century. Let me say only that it is a call within a call, that basic to my vocation [is] my baptism and the attendant commitment to "not be ashamed to confess the faith of Christ crucified, and manfully (sic!) to fight under his banner. . . ." To be a priest is to be recognized within the Christian community as a person for others—a rallier of the troops in the fight we share. I find in that role a tremendous joy and a sobering obligation. It is not a role one chooses but a role for which one is chosen by God and acknowledged by the community.

Perhaps the best way to explain my voice in the night is to share the history of my own call. Read it in the knowledge that it is one person's story and in no way "representative" of women called to priesthood. It is simply my perception of how God has acted in my life.

I was baptized at the age of eleven because my thirteen-year-old brother was ready for confirmation and our parents, never great churchgoers, had not gotten around to having us baptized as infants. My brother remembers the occasion with acute embarrassment and saw to it that his own children were baptized as infants not because he is religious but so that "they'll never have to stand there with all those babies." I, on the other hand, remember feeling profoundly different after the experience and wondering if there might not be a commitment there that I would later be called to act on.

I was not active in church as a teenager or in college. Though nominally an Episcopalian, I got into an altercation with my college because I left blank the question on religion on a form they sent me after I had been accepted. They wrote back that they had to know my religion to put me with a compatible roommate. Sensing a subtle inquiry into whether I was Jewish, I wrote them a long essay about the oneness of God and the harmony of the universe. Puzzled, they put me with a Quaker roommate. As they had hoped, she and I struggled long with our religious questions.

When I was graduated from college, I went to work as a Girl Scout professional worker rather than for the government because I was aware I wanted to work with people rather than ideas. After I had been working about a year, I went home to visit my parents. The rector of our church, a long-time, close friend of the family, dropped by one morning and startled both my mother and me by announcing he had come to pay a "pastoral call" on me. My mother retreated in some puzzlement to her gardening and he and I sat rather formally in the living room. To my amazement he began by announcing that I should be working for the church and that he thought I knew it. Since I had not given it a conscious thought until that moment, I was even more amazed by my immediate response. "Yes," I responded, "I know that, but I can not and will not work for an organization that treats women as miserably as the Episcopal Church does." His response was a sorrowful nod. The most competent member of his staff was an older Director of Religious Education, a widow who, we both knew, made less than the twenty-five-year-old curate and could expect nothing better in the church despite her skill and long experience. He said no more about my working for the church.

He had raised the subject, however, and as I struggled with what to do with my life the church was in the back of my mind. At that time only one Episcopal seminary admitted women to the Bachelor of Divinity program and I actually got up enough interest to go there and inquire, but was told by a woman in the office that what I was interested in was evening courses for laypeople.

Knowing from my scout work in the inner-city of Hartford, Connecticut, that my future probably lay with the oppressed, I decided to spend a summer finding out what life was like for native Americans.

Since the only group I knew that did any work with Indians in my home state of Minnesota was the Episcopal Church, I asked what was available and ended up in a seminarian training program as a resource person on educational techniques for small rural churches. That summer exposed me to the church at work in small-town America, in both Indian and white communities. While it convinced me further that I had a vocation to work with people in the name of Christ, it also reinforced my observation that there was no place for women in professional ministry in the Episcopal Church.

After another year of traveling and teaching in a ghetto high school, I knew it was time to go to graduate school. I went back to the seminary and insisted that the women in the office give me a regular application and let me talk with a faculty member. I applied also to social work school, realizing that, for a woman, was the only practical approach to ministry. By the fall of 1961 I had been accepted at the seminary and also at a social work school halfway across the country. The night before the seminary was to open, I sat with my sister and debated my quandary. Seminary was what I wanted, but I did not want to end up jobless or underemployed like every woman I had ever met who worked for the church. My sister suggested I go over to the seminary the next day just to see if I liked it. If I did not I could drive to the social work school and be there in time for its opening which was five days later. So, on my twenty-fifth birthday, in the midst of a hurricane, I entered Episcopal Theological School. I stayed.

It was clear to me that the only way to avoid being taken advantage of by the church I proposed to serve was to have a skill that was marketable both within and without the institution. So, after a year of seminary I entered social work school as a part-time student and worked on both my B.D. and M.S.W. degrees. When I had both degrees in the spring of 1965, the most promising job I found was to be part of an ecumenical team ministry in a Presbyterian parish in the inner-city in St. Paul, Minnesota. It was an exciting place to be, and though I felt somewhat hampered by my lack of ordination it seemed more important to maintain the ecumenical nature of our ministry by remaining an Episcopalian. Part of my job was to maintain contact with the three Episcopal churches in the neighborhood and to encourage their involvement in neighborhood projects. Word got back to me that the faculty at Episcopal Theological Seminary had heard false rumors that I had been ordained in the Presbyterian church and that they were delighted because it had long been clear that I should be ordained. I began to think for the first time that my ministry might someday include insisting that the Episcopal Church face up to its discrimination against women instead of cheerfully sending its promising women on to other denominations.

Before going to St. Paul, when I was job-hunting in the early months of 1965, a seminary friend of mine put me in touch with his bishop, whom he admired greatly for the pastoral assistance he had received from him in his decision not to be ordained. I had heard about Bishop DeWitt's exciting urban ministry in Philadelphia and I wanted to talk with him about my being a part of it. He was very discouraging because I was a woman, and told me he would take no more women churchworkers in his diocese because he had a canonical responsibility for women workers but no practical power to be of any assistance to them. He urged me to make my career in social work and avoid entanglements with a church that could only disappoint me.

In the spring of 1967, I was offered a job as a welfare rights organizer in a social welfare agency in Philadelphia. It was an exciting opportunity for the kind of social change ministry I was interested in and, though it was not a church-related job, there was high interest in the project in the religious community in Philadelphia. While in Philadelphia interviewing for the job, I called Bishop DeWitt who remembered me well and again warned me that there was nothing in the church for me. He would welcome me to his diocese as a social worker, but I must understand there was no place for me in the church. I took the job.

Eighteen months later, the Philadelphia Welfare Rights Organization was launched and autonomous and no longer needed the help of white social workers. Because of the community organizing skills I had developed, I was offered a job on Bishop DeWitt's staff as "suburban missioner," that is a liaison person for suburban Episcopalians who wanted to work on urban problems. Again Bishop DeWitt and I had a conversation about women and the church. He wanted me to join his staff, but he still felt there was no future for me in the church and was concerned that I should be building my career in social work instead. I suggested that my future was no more precarious than that of another member of his staff who was highly controversial and unpopular with many church people. He replied "His situation is different—he's a priest."

I served as Bishop DeWitt's suburban missioner from 1968 until 1972. In the spring of 1970 a group of women in the Episcopal Peace Fellowship decided it was time for Episcopal women to discuss their situation as women in the church. They called a conference on that subject at Graymoor Ecumenical Center. About sixty women attended and came away from a stimulating weekend having authored a statement calling for opportunity for women to serve in the church at every level including the priesthood and episcopate.

After the Graymoor conference, I decided that the time had come to face up to the fact that God had been steadily pushing me toward ordained ministry for many years and that, despite my resistance, here I was unaccountably still in the Episcopal Church. I went to see Bishop DeWitt about ordination. All my arguments went unused when his immediate response was that he no longer had any doubts about the ordination of women—the only question left was how and when. He helped me begin the application process.

I attended the 1970 General Convention in Houston as a postulant for Holy Orders in the Diocese of Pennsylvania. There were four women at that convention who declared their call to priesthood. When the convention clarified the canons with regard to women's eligibility for the diaconate at least, I proceeded with my postulancy and was ordained deacon in the spring of 1971.

At the Houston convention, it became clear to me that there were large numbers of Episcopal women who felt called to priesthood, but had never dared speak of it before. My first experience with a woman confiding to me about her vocation occurred at Houston. It also became clear at that convention that many laywomen saw the church's non-ordination of women as a sign of their own second-class citizenship.

In January 1972, I took a leave of absence as suburban missioner and began a two-year project as a consultant to women in seminaries. Immediately after the Houston convention, the number of women in Episcopal seminaries began rising and the church needed some preparation for this influx of women. In the course of my seminary work, two of my students surveyed the women graduates of Episcopal seminaries since 1960 and found what I had suspected. Most of the women reported that their seminary years had been great, but the church had been unable to find them satisfying work after graduation. My own research at the seminaries yielded similar data. While our seminaries had many women students, there were very few women faculty, administrators, or trustees.

After the General Convention in Louisville in 1973 ignored the presence of about fifty women who declared their call to priesthood and again refused to deal with the question, I began to be discouraged. I had seen two General Conventions turn away from women in priesthood because in terms of church politics it looked as though it would be more trouble to ordain us than not. I also knew it had taken twenty-five years for the General Convention to approve the seating of women as lay deputies due to its inequitable voting system and the parliamentary delays of the minority that opposed such a move. I saw the grim prospect of the ordination [of women] becoming a perennial issue at General Convention and hundreds of women being diverted from the ministries to which they were called to fight over whether they were called at all. When the Louisville Convention ended with the call for yet another study of the ordination of women it became clear that the route of General Convention approval was the route of delay unacceptable to women but even more unacceptable to the God who was calling us to ordained ministry.

Therefore, when the opportunity to be ordained priest in July of 1974 arose, there was no choice for me but to go ahead. In looking back over my life I see that God has called me to different tasks at different times. It became clear to me in July 1974 that my vocation for now is to try to get the Episcopal Church to face up to its non-ordination of women and what that says about the church to the world it seeks to serve. Since my ordination the conviction has grown that my ten sisters and I are insisting on our vocations now so that other women will not have to spend their ministries in futile self-justification. With the acceptance of women priests, we are also hopeful that the church can gain credibility with the women and men of the world who cannot take seriously an institution that discriminates against women in fact, however noble its rhetoric.

So, as I said at the beginning, I have seen the ordination of women. I resisted the call to ordained ministry in my own life for a long time because I felt I had better things to do than fight the Episcopal Church. When I owned my call, I tried in very ladylike and reasonable ways to convince the church that women could be and, indeed, were called. Finally it became necessary to act on the call despite the church's desire to delay.

The time for argument and apology about the ordination of women to the priesthood is over. Women have been ordained and are functioning as priests and the community is being nourished, the troops are being rallied through their ministries. Like Samuel, women are nudging old Eli—the priestly guard of the sacred things, the church—for the third time. We can only pray that the church, like Eli, will, finally, realize what is happening and respond, "It is the Lord; let him do what seems good to him."

Jonathan Daniels

Militant Saint

Sermon Preached at Eucharist Commemorating
Jonathan Daniels, St. John's Chapel, Episcopal Divinity School,
Cambridge, Massachusetts (March 20, 1975)

Ten years ago this month, a number of seminary students and faculty joined thousands of other Americans in answering the call of Dr. Martin Luther King [Jr.] to come to Selma, Alabama, and march for freedom and voting rights from Selma to Montgomery. When the march ended most of them came home to Cambridge. However, two of those students, Judith Upham (Episcopal Theological School, class of 1967) and Jonathan Daniels (E.T.S., class of 1966) decided to stay on in Selma and continue their civil rights work. With the permission of the faculty they completed their academic work for that term while continuing to live and work in Selma.

Their work that spring involved organizing the ongoing voting rights campaign in the Black community and at the same time attempting to communicate with white Episcopalians in Selma. Every Sunday Judy and Jon came to St. Paul's Episcopal Church in Selma accompanied by a few Black youngsters. They were regularly insulted by the ushers and then seated at the back of the church so that the Blacks would be the last to receive communion.

In August, Jon was shot and killed in the nearby town of Hayneville, Alabama, as he and a small group of other people approached a crossroads store to buy a coke. They were part of a larger group of Blacks and whites who had been arrested a week earlier attempting to register Black voters in Hayneville. Earlier that afternoon the group had been suddenly and inexplicably released from the county jail and their supporters in Selma who would have come to pick them up had not been notified. Jon and a young Roman Catholic priest were shot as they approached the store by a man on the store porch. Judy had gone back to her home in St. Louis for a few weeks and so had not been with the group in Hayneville. She had planned to return to Selma and pick up Jon to return for the fall term in Cambridge.

Briefly, that is the story of Jonathan Daniels, Episcopal Divinity School's most recent and notable martyr. Questions remain about those days, both for those who knew Jon and Judy and for those who didn't. The most nagging of those questions is why? Why did Jon and Judy stay in Selma after all the other Yankees went home? Why did they risk death and create hatred day after day for six months by antagonizing their fellow white Episcopalians, endangering by their very presence their Black friends, and generally "polarizing" that community? In the words of the Collect and Epistle we have just heard, what were the reasons for the hope that was in them?

The senior senator from New Hampshire, Jon's home state, thought he knew. In a speech on the floor of the Senate shortly after Jon's death he blamed the "liberal professors" at Harvard and E.T.S. for filling an impressionable young man with crazy ideas. Jon died as a result, the professors stayed in Cambridge. The senator certainly knew whereof he spoke in making that accusation. That is the time-honored way that old men get young men to fight their wars for them.

Many other people have also given reasons for Jon and Judy being in Selma. In fact, after Jon's death there was a great deal of rhetoric produced about it. I've just had occasion to look at some of it again after ten years. Some of it is good and moving, some not. A great deal was written by E.T.S. people, by churchpeople, by civil rights activists. Much of it was written to relieve guilt or to further "the cause." These are important and valid reasons for producing rhetoric, but such rhetoric seldom touches the heart of the matter.

Peter tells us in his Epistle, "be always ready with your defense when you are called to account for the hope that is in you, but make that defense with modesty and respect." I have such a defense ready to account for the things that I do—a whole panoply of reasons for my actions. I like to think that I can make that defense with modesty and respect. The problem I've discovered, however, is that nobody ever asks for that defense. The opportunity to spell out the reasons for our hope almost never arises.

My first TV appearance was in connection with Jon's death. I was asked to go on a number of local newscasts and talk about Jon and to try as his friend to explain what he was doing in Alabama. My remarks had to be brief and simple, for people have learned from TV that anything worth saying can be said in fifteen, twenty, or sixty seconds. I learned from that experience how little people want to or can hear about life and death issues through the electronic media. I simply described Jon as a Christian living out his faith. In a world where everyone's circuits are overloaded and we are all constantly in an over-stimulated condition, our reasons for what we do have to be short and simple.

Fortunately, sisters and brothers, they are. Jon's and Judy's reasons were too. A Christian's reasons for the hope that is in us can be simply and succinctly stated in three short sentences:

Christ has died.
Christ is risen.
Christ will come again.

Judy and Jon gave their reasons in two brief paragraphs they wrote from Selma. Together they wrote in April 1965:

We are beginning to see as we never saw before that we are truly in the world and yet ultimately not of it. For through the bramble bush (a good E.T.S. image) of doubt and fear . . . we are groping our way to the realization that above all else, we are called to be saints. That is the mission of the Church everywhere. And in this Selma, Alabama is like all the world: it needs the life and witness of militant saints.

Judy, writing in January 1966 told why they had stayed. Anyone who knows Judy knows her to be a sensible, down to earth person, and will appreciate that in the first reason she gives. They stayed because they missed the bus back to Cambridge. Anyone who knew Jon will appreciate her explanation as to why they missed it—Jon lost track of time because he was deep in conversation with someone.

But having missed the bus they had the opportunity to reflect with others who had decided to stay. Judy explains:

> There was no real question about our staying. We had, of course, serious questions about the probability of any action being effective, but the issue seemed to be not effectiveness but faithfulness.

Christian vocation and faithfulness—these are the reasons that Judy and Jon, two ordinary seminarians like ourselves chose to stay in Alabama and lay down their lives for their friends—

Jon quite literally by pushing aside a Black woman to catch in his chest the full blast of a hate-crazed man's shotgun.

Judy by her daily work and risks that spring and summer.

Judy's witness, vocation and faithfulness continue in other times and places. Jon's witness by his death has become a symbol of the hope that is in us all.

Issues change, new "militant saints" emerge, but our hope and the reasons for it remain the same. The old men of Cambridge did not push Jon into his death—if anything Jon's witness pushed a few old men of Cambridge into fresh courage and renewed faithfulness.

We rejoice today in the witness of Jon, whose race is won, and of Judy who continues in faithfulness. And we repeat once more, for any who care to hear, *our* reasons for the great hope that is in *us*: Christ has died. Christ is risen. Christ will come again.

The Challenge of the Churches
Why Bother?

Address to Radcliffe College, 1977

> Sir, a woman preaching is like a dog walking on his hind legs. It is
> not done well: but you are surprised to find it done at all.
> Samuel Johnson (Boswell's *Life*, for the year 1763)

After over two hundred years Dr. Johnson's famous remark is still
quoted to and about women ministers. In part it is incorrect—women
preaching do it very well indeed. But the surprise to find it done at
all remains. In 1977 the surprise is not that a woman should *dare* to
preach, but rather that she should *bother* to do so.

Recently I was stopped in Harvard Square by a fellow graduate of
my seminary—an older man who was eager to introduce me to his wife
as a fellow Radcliffe graduate. Her immediate response to me was to
remark, "Oh, so we lost you to religion." She could not understand how
an educated woman could be part of an institution so notoriously hostile to the aspirations of women as the Christian church. Her attitude is
shared by most of the leadership of the women's movement as well as
by a good number of other thoughtful people of both sexes. Sometimes
I share it myself.

On July 29, 1974, Katrina Welles Swanson, '56, and I, along with
nine other women were ordained Episcopal priests at the Church of the
Advocate in Philadelphia. (Mary Brunton Adebonojo '56, a member of
that parish has since been ordained there as well.) We eleven were the
first Anglican women priests in the western hemisphere. There was no
canon law forbidding the ordination of women, but two of the Episcopal

Church's recent General Conventions in 1970 and 1973 had narrowly defeated attempts to change the canons to specifically include women. We women felt we had exhausted the political process for change. We knew that a minority of convention delegates could delay women's ordination indefinitely through parliamentary maneuvers and by calling for new "studies" of the question periodically. The first such study had been done in 1919 and reached essentially the same conclusions as the latest done in 1972. Such procedures had delayed the seating of laywomen as delegates to General Conventions from the time the matter first came up in 1946 until women were seated in 1970. Many of us had felt called to priesthood for many years. The Rev. Dr. Jeanette Piccard, renowned balloonist and educator, at age 79 had been conscious of her vocation from the time she was eleven years old. All eleven of us were qualified, educated, and certified for priestly ordination and had served as deacons the requisite length of time. The three bishops who ordained us did so without the permission of our own local bishops, a clear "irregularity" according to canon law, but one they felt the circumstances—the church's impasse on women's ordination—justified.

In August 1974, the American Episcopal bishops declared our ordinations "invalid," rather than merely "irregular," a decision that proved untenable for them both theologically and practically. Theologically, the decision was hard to defend since the ordinations met the four classic tests for validity of orders in the catholic tradition. Practically, the decision proved unwise in that it further undermined the already waning authority of bishops since it was three of their number who had done the ordaining.

A year later in September 1975, four more women deacons were ordained to the priesthood in Washington, D.C. by yet another bishop. After another year of turmoil, punctuated by increasing acceptance of the ministry of the women priests by the laity; two ecclesiastical trials of male priests who had welcomed the women to their parishes; and increasing ridicule of the Episcopal hierarchy by the media, the next General Convention voted in the fall of 1976 to explicitly open all orders of clergy to women on the same basis as men. Though the controversy continues, with a few parishes seceding from the church and a number of bishops vowing never to ordain or accept women priests, the fifteen women ordained before 1976 have quietly been welcomed by their bishops as priests without re-ordination and other women continue to be ordained. At this writing, there are over one hundred women priests in the Episcopal Church, a small number in comparison to the twelve thousand male priests, but a remarkable number in view of the fact that a year ago there were only fifteen "irregularly" ordained women priests, engaged in a sort of guerilla warfare with the ecclesiastical authorities.

The Philadelphia ordinations did not mark the beginning of women's efforts to take a fuller role in the ministry of the Episcopal Church; nor did the decision of 1976 mark an end to those efforts. Employment opportunities for clergywomen are scarce and hostility in some quarters remains strong. Our sister ministers in other denominations are familiar with these persistent problems.

Women have been seeking ordination in the Anglican tradition for over one hundred years. While women were ordained in a number of denominations in the U.S.A. in the nineteenth century, the Anglican response to the awakening vocations of women was the re-introduction of two ancient religious orders for women, deaconesses, and nuns. It was understood that women in either order remained laywomen. In the 1950s and early 1970s, the barriers to women's ordination fell in most American churches. By 1974, only the Episcopalians, Roman Catholics and Orthodox among the major Christian denominations categorically denied ordination to women. Reform and Reconstructionist Judaism had also admitted a few women as rabbis.

The "how" of women's ordination in the Episcopal Church is a long and continuing story. The "why" of women's ordination at this late date in Christian history is to me the more interesting question. As in the larger women's movement, the struggle in the churches has its heroines and heroes. Why they have bothered and continue to bother is the significant part of the story.

First, it was and remains a matter of simple justice. Dr. Charles V. Willie of the Harvard Graduate School of Education said it plainly in his sermon at the Philadelphia ordinations and subsequently at the first celebration of the Eucharist by women priests in October 1974, when he asserted "God is an equal opportunity employer." Dr. Willie was, at the time of the Philadelphia ordinations, the highest ranking layman in the Episcopal Church as vice-president of the General Convention's house of deputies. He resigned that office in protest when the bishops declared the ordinations invalid.

A second and related reason is our theological understanding of the importance to Christians of freedom and equality. The New Testament carries the good news that there is neither Jew nor Greek, slave nor free, male nor female, but we are all one in Christ. The church has long celebrated our equality in the sacrament of baptism as a sign of our oneness in Christ. It is unreasonable to baptize both men and women but to ordain only men. Of course not all Christians are called to ordination, but those who do feel called should be given the opportunity to test that call.

Yet even if we admit the justice and theological necessity of ordaining women, we still have not answered the question of why women should seek ordination. Aside from questions of vocation and personal belief, is there any reason for women to bother with the church, especially to seek to join the ranks of the clergy? This is a question of great concern to Roman Catholic women who are struggling with the dilemma of ordination. Yes, they say, women should be ordained, but would we or the church gain anything by our joining an antiquated and sexist hierarchy? Would we not be joining the enemy? Women seeking to join the armed services or competing for Rhodes scholarships or entering Harvard University must ask themselves the same question. Why should women concerned about other women join the very forces that traditionally have been most misogynistic?

In the case of the churches I think there are two compelling reasons to bother. The first is the symbolic value of women as clergy. Most church-going Christians in the U.S., at least sixty percent, are women. Despite the gains in education and opportunity for women over the past hundred years, for many women the church is still the primary outlet for their energies outside the home. "Kinder, Küche, Kirche" remains a way of life for many and "kirche" is as close to the world as many women can get. If these women and their daughters see other women in positions of leadership in church, perhaps their own aspirations and self-image will be changed. Possibly. If a woman is interested in reaching her sisters, the churches are a good place to begin.

The second reason is related to the first. Despite their dwindling memberships, the churches still have enormous influence in matters considered to be "moral" issues. Many of these acknowledged "moral" issues are also women's issues. The churches have had a great deal to say on questions of sexuality, abortion, and marriage. Even the ERA is seen by many as a "moral" issue, since it allegedly threatens traditional family structures. It is ironic that decisions about issues that are vital to women are so often made by church bodies dominated by men (often celibate men at that). As Dr. Mary Daly, feminist philosopher, has remarked, 100 percent of the people needing abortions are women while 100 percent of the Roman Catholic bishops deciding that abortion is unnecessary and immoral are men. As long as church councils are making judgments about women's issues, women must insist on being included in the deliberations.

So women concerned about women have reason to bother with preaching and ordination. But like women pioneering in any field that has been male-dominated we need to be especially vigilant about the dangers of becoming part of rather than merely the object of the councils of the church. The great danger for women in ministry is the danger of "out-clericalizing" the male clergy. If we allow ourselves to become part of the system as it is, we will simply compound the oppression of women. By becoming tokens we take the pressure off the institution to change its view of women in any profound way. Like Radcliffe women, we must constantly remember that Harvard and the churches are lucky to have us. The experience and viewpoint we bring as women to the institutions we would join are not handicaps to be overcome but gifts to strengthen our common endeavor.

Women have a long tradition in ministry—probably the oldest fragment of the Bible is the victory song of the women led by Miriam after the crossing of the Red Sea (Exodus 15:21). Women ministers of all denominations, and there are many Radcliffe women among us, face the challenge of keeping alive our female heritage and our obligation to insist on the God-given dignity of all persons. In order to do this we must stay in contact with each other and avoid the temptation to become the token woman minister who gets along "exceptionally" well with the men.

Our numbers are increasing and our reforming, perhaps revolutionizing, task is clear. We are bothering to preach, it is done well. As a result the churches are healthier places for women and girls.

Sermon Preached at the Ordination of Sandra Hughes Boyd to the Priesthood

Christ Church, Cambridge, Massachusetts (April 21, 1979)

In a few minutes Bishop McGehee will address Sandy as follows:

> My sister, the Church is the family of God, the body of Christ, and the temple of the Holy Spirit. All baptized people are called to make Christ known as Savior and Lord, and to share in the renewing of his world. Now you are called to work as a pastor, priest, and teacher, together with your bishop and fellow presbyters, to take your share in the councils of the Church.

That paragraph bothers me, especially the last sentence. When I was ordained deacon, my share in the governance of the Church was not mentioned, nor were my fellow deacons referred to. When I was confirmed, the councils of the Church did not come up at all. Does this paragraph infer that it is only priests and bishops who have voice in the way the Church is run? What then is the ministry of deacons and laypeople?

On re-reading that paragraph I am relieved to realize that it only says we priests are "to take our share" in those councils and I relax a bit. But it is descriptions such as this that lead us to see priesthood as an elitist band—until very recently a band of brothers. All too often and too easily priests have become a caste in the Church. Indeed, the very word "hierarchy" means the rule of the priest.

It is not difficult to understand how this has happened. Priests dress differently and are front and center in our rituals. Only they may do certain things. They are vested with a certain authority that goes with the office rather than coming from the person.

All those things mean that we priests are in danger of taking ourselves too seriously—of acting as though we ourselves were holy. Or sometimes falling all over ourselves to demonstrate that we are regular folks who can joke and swear like everybody else despite our priestly office. The laity aid and abet us in this danger by treating us differently and deferentially when we are ordained.

The thing we need to remind ourselves of is that the ministry of priests is peculiar (as is every ministry) but those who exercise it are no holier than the rest of humanity. What the peculiar ministry of priests is is a question newly open for discussion in our day—it may well be changing. But for the time being we remain a church with an ordered ministry. As new classes of persons enter those orders old ideas about them change, but the orders remain.

The role of priests is peculiar but not especially blessed. Sainthood and beatitude are open to all—laity, deacons, priests and bishops. God doesn't call us to priesthood because we're especially good or even especially faithful. God calls us to priesthood because we're available.

In this regard the experience of Isaiah that Hayden read to us is instructive. God called Isaiah through a vision of the Holy One—an awesome vision in a room filled with smoke and the flapping of wings of the terrifying Cherubim. Isaiah reacted as we might with despair and terror. "Woe is me, for I am a person of unclean lips and I dwell among a people of unclean lips." In other words I am not worthy of the ministry you ask me to perform. But God cannot be put off and remedies the situation, painfully but unarguably, with a burning coal and then asks—as God often asks—"who shall we send? Who will go for us? Quietly, Isaiah replies, "here am I, send me." God seeks a messenger. Isaiah, though protesting his unworthiness, volunteers his availability—and he is henceforth in the service of the Lord.

Unworthy as we all are—diverse as we are—we answer God's call, peculiar and different for each of us, with this same simple statement of availability—here am I, send me. So God does, and on occasions such as confirmations and ordinations the Church acknowledges the call and the response.

That brings me to a second point about our calling, especially the calling to those of us who are priests. We are a motley crew. We bring different gifts, talents, strengths, and weaknesses to our calling. Each of us brings her or his peculiar self to this ministry.

But for all that diversity, the words the bishop will say remind us of another thing about priests—we are always lumped with our "fellow presbyters." Priesthood is not a solo ministry. That is why the priests present will join in the laying on of hands in a few minutes. The priests here this morning will represent our 160 sisters and 17,000 brothers who share the priesthood in this time and in this branch of Christ's church. We will symbolically share with Sandy the power and the burden of the priesthood.

But it is not just the priests here who will share in that power and burden. One of the priestly vows that Sandy will soon assent to is "to be a faithful pastor to all who she is called to serve, laboring together with them and with her fellow ministers to build up the family of God."

Paul, in the passage Peggy read from Ephesians, uses imagery of the way the parts of a human body work together for the functioning of the whole to make the point that all of us have our part in the mission of the church. I tend to be suspicious of Paul's use of body imagery—all too often it has been used, even by whole societies, to justify oppression. Certain groups have often said to others, "We're a body—we'll be the head and you folks can be the feet." The point of such imagery is not who will be what part—rather it is that our mission is of a piece—an organic whole to which we all contribute. Bishops, priests, deacons, laypersons are not more nor less than servants and fellow laborers with the whole people of Christ. Paul makes the further point that when we all work together "we shall at last attain the unity inherent in our faith to grow up in Christ." We—not I but we—all of us together will finally be adults in the faith.

And to be adults in the faith—to build up the family of God—is all for the larger purpose of spreading the good news of Jesus—the news that God has vindicated our lord and we and everyone are thereby healed and freed. The poor, the oppressed, the captives of this world are loved and cherished by our God. We all—deacons, bishops, laypersons, priests—are called together to spread that word and make it real in the world.

Sandy, today is an important day for you. It's the culmination of a dream and a quest that have led you places you never suspected existed when you were in Council Bluffs, or Colorado Springs, or Minneapolis, or Columbus. Perhaps you began to know in Rochester. In any case, today the church recognizes the priesthood you claim. You don't become a priest today—I have seen you work as a pastor in my livingroom—as a priest in a small bare room in a mental hospital—as a teacher in the classroom. And I have seen you take your share (some would say more than your share) in the councils of the church.

Today we make that priesthood public—perhaps we validate it like a parking sticker or a driver's license. But that validation will not change you or the relationships with which you struggle and in which you rejoice.

You are a person who expects much of yourself and of others. Whatever you do, you strive to do well. But my warning to you this morning is that there is no way to do priesthood well. It is useless to strive to be a "good" priest—such striving often leads to the very elitism and self-importance you so deplore. All you can do is continue to listen for God's word—continue to be available to do God's will, not well, but as best you can.

And so, sister—two words of advice—one from an ancient Greek philosopher—one from a nineteenth century feminist. First, know yourself—know who Sandy is and accept her as she is. Second, trust in God—She will provide. Amen.

Women in the Episcopal Diaconate and Priesthood

An Unrecognized Shared History

Paper Presented at the Sixth Berkshire Conference
on the History of Women, Smith College,
Northampton, Massachusetts (June 1–3, 1984)

When Anglican women began agitating seriously for admittance to the priesthood (about 1970 in the United States and briefly in the early 1940s in China), there was very little identification with the deaconesses and less recollection of the nineteenth-century struggle of English and American church women to become deaconesses. When American Episcopal women gathered in April 1970 to discuss our role in our church, the impetus for that meeting was not any recollection of the struggle of deaconesses, missionaries and church workers to find recognition and opportunities for ministry over the last century. It was rather the experience of marginalization that many of us had had in the civil rights and peace movements of the 1960s. Specifically that meeting, which I would name as the beginning of the movement for women's ordination that culminated in our church's recognition of women priests in 1977, was called by women active in the Episcopal Peace Fellowship who had made the connection between the marginalization of women in the peace movement and our marginalization in the church itself. They simply mailed a notice of meeting to discuss women's role in the church to all women on their mailing list and about sixty of us showed up.

Of that sixty, a few of us were seminary-educated women who had felt a vocation to ordained ministry and had taken advantage of the fact that Episcopal and nondenominational seminaries had gradually opened their MDiv degree programs to women over the post-war years. The Episcopal Church had first felt the need for seminary-trained women workers in the boom years of the late 50s and early 60s. Later, the seminaries had felt the need for paying students when the clergy job market began to shrink in the 1960s. My own seminary, Episcopal Theological School (ETS) in Cambridge, Massachusetts, had opened its ministerial training program to women in 1959 with great fanfare about the church's need for theologically-educated women workers. The question of women's ordination was strenuously avoided, but when pushed the seminary faculty claimed no position on that question.

When I was a student at ETS in the early 1960s it was very clear to me that whatever form my ministry would take I would never consider becoming a deaconess. The church canons described deaconesses as women "of devout character" with "a high school education" who were to be "set apart" for a particular ministry under the direction of a bishop. They took vows, though not life vows, and could serve as deaconesses only as long as they remained unmarried. It was never suggested to me that I might find my place in the church as a deaconess and certainly it was never whispered that deaconesses were in any sense ordained. If I thought about deaconesses at all it was as a nineteenth-century phenomenon and all I knew about the nineteenth-century deaconesses was that they had been exploited at home and abroad as domestic and foreign missionaries. Somewhere I had picked up the interesting bit of trivia that deaconesses who worked with Native Americans wore grey instead of navy blue uniforms because Native Americans saw navy blue as the color of the hated U.S. Cavalry.

By the time I first met any deaconesses at the church's General Convention in 1970 there were only about seventy-five of them left and nearly half of those were of retirement age or beyond. However in meeting these women I began to realize for the first time what intrepid and valiant souls they were and to appreciate the daring and devoted lives they had led. Many of them were understandably hostile to the women clamoring for priesthood. They felt trivialized and forgotten in the general rush toward what they perceived as the self-aggrandizement of women seeking priesthood.

Church officials of the late nineteenth century had hoped the restored female diaconate would be the answer to the "woman problem." Twentieth-century church officials had hoped that declaring deaconesses to be within the diaconate (i.e., ordained to be deacons exactly as male deacons are) would be the answer to that problem, too, and indeed in many parts of the Anglican Communion that move is still being debated. But, the church's ambivalence toward women meant that no matter how it was framed a separate and distinct ministry for women never had a chance to be taken seriously. During the ordination struggle of the early 1970s I met a woman English professor, then retired, who had trained in her youth at St. Faith's House in New York City, a training school for deaconesses and women church workers. She had debated becoming a deaconess but found it vaguely unsatisfying until she attended the "setting apart" of one of her classmates. When a priest swept into the sacristy before that service and announced that he had arrived to participate in the "setting aside" of Miss Smith, she knew why she didn't choose to serve as a deaconess. She was finally ordained deacon in 1973 and served as a priest for a few years before her death in 1980.

Furthermore, the diaconate could never be taken seriously as an answer to the woman problem because the diaconate itself, male or female, was seen as a secondary and subservient office in the church at large. In the catholic tradition the diaconate (until 1968 the male diaconate) has been since ancient times an ordained ministry, the first of the three major and indelible orders in the church—deacon, priest and bishop. All priests and bishops are also deacons, having been ordained to that office along the way. Perhaps this is the reason that deaconesses took hold more readily in more protestant churches—there never was any question that deaconesses (and deacons) were laypeople. In the Anglican, Orthodox, and Roman Catholic churches deacons have always been considered clergy, hence a parallel order for women has led to confusion as to whether the women were ordained or lay. The result of this confusion was that deaconesses were never clearly defined or widely accepted as either.

In any case, even male deacons were considered lesser ministers than priests or bishops. Let me read to you part of the concluding prayer from the service for the ordination of deacons in the 1928 Book of Common Prayer, in use in the Episcopal Church until 1979.

"In regard to the newly ordained deacons we pray to God to . . . Make them . . . to be modest, humble and constant in their Ministration, to have a ready will to observe all spiritual Discipline; that they . . . may so well behave themselves in this inferior Office that they may be found worthy to be called unto the higher Ministries in Thy Church." This passage summarizes both the transitory and the inferior nature of the diaconate as the church regards the office. Furthermore, deacons are still not allowed to serve as deputies to General Conventions of the Church in either the clergy or the lay orders.

Yet it was the admission of women to the diaconate in 1970 and the declaration that deaconesses were considered ordained in the same way male deacons were that opened the door to women in the priesthood of the Episcopal Church. The move to change the canon on deaconesses and to admit women as deacons came not from the people urging women's ordination to the priesthood but from the small group of devout women, mostly elderly and conservative who were the national conference of deaconesses by 1970. The Lambeth Conference (a world gathering of Anglican bishops that meets every ten years at Lambeth Palace in London) of 1968 had decreed that national churches could declare women eligible to be ordained deacons. Furthermore, deaconesses who had been set apart by the laying on of hands could be considered ordained deacons. A number of national churches (Hong Kong, Canada, New Zealand, Kenya and Burma) had taken this step by 1970. The American deaconesses brought a resolution to the 1970 General Convention of the Episcopal Church to the effect that deaconesses so ordered (virtually all of them then living) be declared deacons and that men and women deacons henceforth meet the same educational and other requirements.

The 1970 General Convention had been dominated by the debate over a resolution from an entirely different source that women be ordained to all orders of ministry (deacon, priest and bishop). When that resolution was narrowly defeated in the clergy order there was great disappointment and anger among women, a handful of whom had just been seated as lay deputies after a twenty-five-year debate on that question. The resolution from the deaconesses came to convention floor on the very last day of the meeting and was approved over-whelmingly by deputies eager to find a solution to the woman problem and mollify the many angry women surrounding them. The diaconate as booby prize as it were. The deaconesses were elated to have been taken seriously and given official status as ordained women at last.

1970 was the point at which the deaconesses' history and the history of those working for the full ordination of women came together. It was through the efforts of the deaconesses that women became eligible to be ordained deacons. I remember reading a clipping from the *New York Times* about that vote posted on a bulletin board at Haverford College and thinking, "Well, that's the ballgame. We've won and women will be ordained to all orders within five years."

The reason I was so buoyed by that move was more theological than political, though I was even then in the thick of the politics that ultimately led to the ordination of women priests. Theologically, the ordained ministry cannot be divided—one cannot argue that women are unfit for one form of indelible ordination and not another. The opponents of women's ordination saw that and argued vociferously but vainly that women could not be deacons any more than they could be priests or bishops because the key theological question, going back even to Aquinas, was whether women were "proper matter" to receive indelible ordination. If they could be ordained deacon that question was settled.

And so it was the deaconesses who drove the opening wedge for women to be ordained priests in the Episcopal Church. That was certainly not their intention. I invited two elderly deaconesses to my ordination as a deacon in June 1971 and to our mutual distress they were shocked and offended by the emphasis in that service that all seven of us (I was ordained with six men) would go on to become priests. That was certainly not the kind of ministry they had in mind for me. I was only beginning to realize what had come before me in the way of women's ministry and they were only beginning to sense what lay ahead.

By the 1973 General Convention there were about forty-five newly-ordained women deacons lobbying for ordination of women to the priesthood. The former deaconesses, now by fiat also deacons, were divided in their opinion on whether women should be priests, but they did not allow the opposition to capitalize on their uncertainty and those opposed remained silent. Again we were very conscious of our shared history as women oppressed by the church we had loved and served so long.

The history of the struggle of women to be ordained priests in the Episcopal Church is another long and complicated one. I would refer you to an article of mine in the current issue of the *Journal of Ecumenical Studies* (Vol. 20, no. 4, Fall 1983), "How We Brought the Good News from Graymoor to Minneapolis: An Episcopal Paradigm." For purposes of this paper let it suffice to say that the resolution to ordain women priests and deacons was again defeated at the 1973 Convention. As a result and due to a careful look at how profound changes in the life of the church occur, eleven women deacons found three retired and resigned bishops who were willing to ordain them priests in the summer of 1974 without waiting for a change in canon law. Cries of outrage from the bishops and a declaration that no ordinations had occurred followed within a month. Within another two months the women began functioning publically as priests and within a year two male priests had been tried and convicted in ecclesiastical courts of disobeying their bishops by allowing women priests to celebrate the Eucharist in their parishes. In the fall of 1975 another retired bishop ordained four more women deacons to the priesthood and by the fall of 1976 the next General Convention of the Episcopal Church changed canon law to permit the ordination of women as priests and bishops beginning January 1, 1977. The bishops in that convention also provided a way in which the 15 women already ordained might be recognized as priests without having to be re-ordained. Interestingly, the first American deaconesses had been recognized in a similar process. Several deaconesses were set apart in two dioceses by individual bishops in 1885 and 1887. The General Convention added a canon permitting the setting apart of deaconesses in 1889. Changes in canon law often follow the bold action of individual dioceses and church members. I refer anyone interested in learning more about the 1974 and 1975 ordinations to a current special issue of *The Witness Magazine* commemorating the tenth anniversary of those events.

As I close I would like to share with you several questions that this morning's look at the history of women in the churches raises for me. First I want to emphasize what I perceive as a discontinuity between the twentieth- and the nineteenth-century battles for the ordination of women. (I am conscious as I write this that it may not be a discontinuity at all, but only a misperception on my part of how those nineteenth-century women saw themselves.) However, I think the American women who won ordination in the late twentieth century differed from our foremothers in that we took ordination as a right rather than receiving it as a gift from the Church.

The history of women's ordination in Canada's Anglican Church is different from ours. There everything was done decently and in order. Indeed after it became possible for women to be ordained priest in 1976, bishops urged deaconesses and laywomen workers on the northern and western frontiers who are known as "bishop's messengers" to seek ordination so they could administer the sacraments in their remote ministries. Most did so, some reluctantly. A U.S. woman priest, meeting several years ago with Canadian women priests, remarked to me afterwards that the Canadian priests seemed much more docile and passive than U.S. priests and suggested that this came from their not having had to defy the church to pursue their ministries.

I wonder, ten years later, if the way we won ordination makes any difference in the way Episcopal women practice the ministerial profession. There are now over five hundred women priests in the U.S. Episcopal Church working in about seventy of our approximately 100 dioceses (through a political compromise misnamed "the conscience clause" bishops and dioceses that disapprove of women priests are not required to ordain or accept them). The church is eager to forget that there was ever any trouble about women priests, hence our history of insisting on ordination before the canons were changed is widely forgotten. Most Episcopalians who know we ordain women (that 500 is less than 5 percent of our total clergy) assume that when women presented themselves for ordination the church accepted them gladly. Women clergy have trouble finding jobs in the church beyond the entry level and tend to move laterally if at all. In terms of the nineteenth-century models for women's diaconate, the familial model is almost nonexistent and the "diocesan-parochial model" prevails everywhere for women priests, except for the handful who are also nuns. Loneliness is also a problem for both female and male priests. Though the canons allow it there are no women bishops.

Yet women priests have made a difference, I think. The seminaries are filled with women, mostly embarking on ministry as a second career. The entering class at the seminary where I teach was 85 percent female this year, most of them older women coming back to school after having pursued other careers. The trustees, alumni and male faculty are alarmed that we are becoming a "ladies' seminary," but the question it raises for me is the exciting and dangerous one of whether ordained ministry is becoming a woman's profession.

The question is dangerous, for the history of professions that have become "women's professions" is not a happy one for women. What that has meant is that these professions (and I have in mind social work, nursing and teaching) have become what is referred to as "semi-professions." Furthermore, as the "rank and file" in these professions has become increasingly female, the leadership has become increasingly male (e.g., heads of agencies, school principals and administrators). I wonder if we are looking to a future in ministry where priests are female and bishops are male.

But the question is also exciting precisely because women may be able to enter the ministerial profession on our own terms and thereby change the way it's practiced. We weren't invited in, indeed, we were kept out for many centuries. Of course that's true of women in all professions, but in ministry the change has happened in our lifetime and the profession has not yet had a chance to absorb women and see to it that we adapt to "professional" values. We are self-conscious about being women in a previously all-male profession and some of us are more eager to change the profession than adapt to "the way things are done."

The challenge for women in ministry is nothing less than to change the ways ministry is done. The symbol of this, I think, is the current struggle of women, ordained and lay, to change the language about God in our worship to reflect the wholeness of humanity, not just the maleness of God and man. The resistance from male clergy comes in professional terms—"it is a violation of my ordination vows to change the language of scripture and liturgy." The question for me is whether women clergy can and will insist on breaking the male professional pattern.

Some signs are discouraging and lead me to envision what I call the *Animal Farm* scenario. You may recall the scene in that book when Orwell's revolutionary animals spy on the pigs supposedly negotiating for them and find they cannot distinguish them from the men with whom they are talking. As women enter male professions we are often more eager to prove we're "professional" by outdoing the men at traditional (i.e., male) marks of the profession. Dressing for success is the most obvious manifestation of this phenomenon, but it is also seen in more serious illustrations. There are a few female deans of seminaries here and there and the report that drifts back to women faculty elsewhere is that they tend to be even less supportive of feminist theologians, faculty and students than male deans. This is due to an entirely understandable effort to prove to their peers that they are true "professionals" and not creatures of the interest groups they represent. The worry among women theological educators that we are educating and ordaining "too many" women is another illustration of our fear of being accused of taking over the profession.

But a few signs are encouraging. Our numbers is one such sign. We may change the way ministry is practiced in spite of ourselves. Women don't command paternal authority the way men do (even when we call ourselves "Mother") and so we are forced into a more collegial and democratic style of leadership.

Finally our history should teach us, if we take the trouble to uncover and remember it, that women have been engaged in ministry for a very long time and that those who have gone before were brave and wise and deserve the respect of our emulation. It is the twentieth-century "profession" of the theologian and ecclesiastical bureaucrat that is the aberration, not the centuries-old "semi-profession" of pastoral care and healing—the history we share with both the nineteenth and the first-century deaconesses.

Fair Harvard's Daughters

Radcliffe Quarterly, 71, no. 3 (September 1985): 41–42

Since I live in Cambridge and work on an academic schedule, I have the privilege of attending Harvard commencement every June, and I try to do that if I can. I attend by television—it's easier on the feet and I always get a good seat. This practice also has the advantage of the college reunion participation we all dream of—where we get a chance to see everybody and what has become of them, but they don't see us in our middle-aged state and they don't have an opportunity to pass judgment on what has become of us.

I was struck as I watched the festival rites by how small a part Radcliffe seemed to play in the proceedings and how few women and minority persons were in evidence. As the camera rolled over the "dignitaries" on the platform, I caught only an occasional glimpse of a woman or a person of color. There was one woman and one non-white among the ten honorary degree recipients. When, I wondered, will the proportion of women and minorities among the people on the platform begin to approach the proportion of such people among those receiving degrees? What does one woman honorary degree recipient out of ten say to those six hundred plus women in the class of 1985 about their futures? Can any of them look forward to being honored someday by their alma mater for their accomplishments?

And then in the afternoon the gathering sang both "Radcliffe Now We Rise to Greet Thee" and "Fair Harvard." The first was stumbled through with embarrassment by both women and men. The second is always moving and was so yesterday in that setting, with both elderly men and young women brushing away a tear as they sang, "Fair Harvard thy sons to thy jubilee throng." It gets to me, too, as I remember crisp fall days along the river. But even as I sing it, I know that I am not Harvard's son, and that by declaring myself such I deny that I am Radcliffe's daughter. Perhaps that is the real reason I always watch the commencement exercises at home. Somehow the message that Harvard really doesn't celebrate its daughters comes across loud and clear—so clear that I don't feel welcome in the yard on commencement day.

Not that I would have us return to the old days. When I graduated from Radcliffe our commencement was held in the Radcliffe quad during a lull in reunion week activities and a few members of the Harvard band and a handful of junior faculty turned up for the event. We told ourselves it was more personal than Harvard commencement—we did receive our diploma from President Jordan after all. But my most lasting memory is of being shunted aside once more from the real life of the university. It was a stage of the long struggle to integrate women into Harvard, and that particular battle has been long won.

Things have changed for the better despite the impression that women are still largely ignored in the Harvard festivities. Radcliffe has been freed to become an advocate for women both in terms of such programs as the Bunting Institute and the Schlesinger Library and the roles of women throughout the university. Radcliffe's publications, the *Radcliffe Quarterly* and *Second Century*, are consistently filled with articles of special interest to women. They report exhaustively on the many areas of scholarship in which women are taking a leading part. Through these programs and excellent publications, Radcliffe remains my primary route of access to Harvard and I am proud of being a Radcliffe graduate.

Rememberers

But alma mater has changed (when in her short history has Radcliffe not been in the process of change?) and perhaps her new role in the university suggests a new role for us as her alumnae—as the women graduates of Harvard University. What is our responsibility to the women of this university, past, present, and future?

First, I think it is up to us to be the rememberers. All of us remember what it was like to be a woman here during different eras. Helen Homans Gilbert '36 spoke to us last year at this service about what it was like in the 1930s. Two years ago Karen Wilk Klein '58 described life here in the 1950s. We all have tales to tell, and it is important that they be told.

Women's history is easily forgotten. Just yesterday I remarked to a young male alumnus of the school where I teach that I had been the first woman student who was allowed to preach in the chapel there, in 1964. He was amazed and horrified that the integration of women there was so recent and so partial. He reminded me that most young men and women don't know very much about women's struggles for equality, either in the nineteenth century or the 1960s.

Our history is precious and I thank Radcliffe for recognizing that in its support of the women's archives at the Schlesinger Library. We who made that history must insist that it be remembered and preserved. When people ask me "Did you go to Harvard?" and I say "yes" rather than recite the whole complicated history of Radcliffe, I always feel a pang of guilt. I notice that young women graduates don't feel that at all but easily refer to themselves as Harvard graduates. The embarrassed giggling that accompanies the singing of the Radcliffe alma mater on commencement day is a small instance of the way women's history gets trivialized and then forgotten. We need to resist that tendency in ourselves and look at our past with the respect and honor it deserves. Certainly, if we don't, no one else will.

Next, our responsibility to the women of this university is to be role models. Many of us are the first, or nearly the first, women in our professions (at least as far as we know, because women's history is so fragile, many "first" of previous generations have been lost and are only now being repeated). Others of us have done exemplary work in the professions women have followed for generations—as mothers, as educators, as homemakers, healers, and caretakers—as nurses and social workers. None of us set out to be role models or first woman-this-or-that. We found ourselves in these positions and did the best we could.

For those of us in professions where we had no female role models, doing the best we could meant doing the job as we had observed men who we admired doing it, in short proving that we were the "best man" for the job. Like being a "son" of fair Harvard, being the "best man" comes easily to us when we have experienced no "best women."

But being the "best man" is a disservice to women coming after us. Could we perhaps instead make common cause with those women to change the professions we've struggled to enter? It is incumbent on us as role models to see that women's gifts—our penchant for humanizing, our habit of addressing particularities rather than abstractions—are taken seriously. Business and the professions could certainly benefit from our insights and our women's experience of the world.

Animal Farm scenario

One of my recurring nightmares about my own profession of ministry is what I call the *Animal Farm* scenario. You may remember the last chapter of George Orwell's *Animal Farm*, where the revolutionary animals send their representatives, the pigs, to negotiate with the farmers. They wait outside for a report, and when none is forthcoming they look in the window and discover to their horror that the pigs have become so thoroughly acclimated to human ways that the other animals can't distinguish them from the men in the farmhouse. After the long struggle to get women ordained I fear a day when we will no longer be able to tell the women clergy from the men. The danger of such assimilation is great. It has happened in other professions, even those now commonly thought of as women's professions. What often follows is a situation where the "rank and file" are largely women, the key administrators largely men. Women priests but men bishops is the prospect for us.

If women enter the public world in great numbers but don't change the way things are done there, then there is really no gain for anyone. Indeed there is a net loss, for the women who used to carry the burden of volunteer community service are no longer available to do that. Being "the best man" is a losing proposition for both women and society.

We who are role models, like it or not, have a responsibility to go in new directions and to help our professions change and grow. We need to value what women have to offer and see that it doesn't get left at home. Role modeling, whether in a hitherto male bastion or as a wife, mother, or volunteer, requires intelligence, imagination, and courage.

But we can do it. We are, after all Radcliffe alumnae, and Radcliffe's whole history has been about transforming a male institution.

In summary, I think our responsibility as alumnae of this university is to value ourselves and other women and to insist that we be taken seriously. We must let Harvard know that an institution that doesn't value women cannot be a true university, for it only acknowledges part of the universe. We need to do whatever we do in the world with the understanding that other women are observing us. We need to be committed to working with those other women to do what we do better. Most of all we need to celebrate each other and rejoice in the company of educated women. Harvard is lucky to have us.

The Great Thing About Mary

The Witness 69, no. 12 (December 1986): 6–8.

A friend sent me an ad recently for a poster she thought I might want to use as a teaching tool. At the center of the poster is an abstract version of a Madonna and child. Surrounding this medallion is the legend, *The great thing about Mary is that her son turned out so well! Alleluia!* My friend thought I might want to use the poster in a quiz; i.e. "What's wrong with the theology here expressed?" But then again, she supposed my students were too sophisticated to take it seriously.

However, the fact that the poster undoubtedly sells well (and not cheaply either—$14.50 mounted in a clear plastic box) makes one wonder if it doesn't reflect the common Christian wisdom. There is clear and specific Dominical teaching to the contrary in the New Testament:

> While he was speaking thus, a woman in the crowd called out "Happy the womb that carried you and the breasts that suckled you!" He rejoined, "No, happy are those who hear the word of God and keep it." (Luke 11:27-28)

Yet many Christians still believe that women are to be judged on the accomplishments of the men they are close to and presumably influence. Popular Mariology may well be summed up in that poster despite the efforts of modern theologians like Hans Küng to honor Mary as the first among believers.

Reflections on the role of Mary in particular and women in general in the Christian church come naturally at Christmastime. They come to me especially at the close of this year as I look back at some poignant milestones involving Anglican women in 1986. In April, an event was held at Canterbury Cathedral honoring the work of Anglican women worldwide. A stirring service recognizing the various ministries of women throughout the Communion was followed by another service that a number of women felt it necessary to boycott as the host church, the Church of England, refused to allow any women priests from other provinces to exercise their sacramental ministry.

In May, a woman was very nearly elected Suffragan Bishop of Washington, but again the sensibilities of the Church of England were invoked and the convention was persuaded to "wait" until after the next Lambeth Conference (a worldwide conference of Anglican bishops held every 10 years in England) scheduled for 1988, so as not to promote "disunity" in the Anglican Communion. In July, the Church of England reaffirmed its ban on allowing women ordained in other Anglican provinces to celebrate Eucharist in English churches and declined to vote on ordaining English women priests until further study could be done. (The first such study was done in 1919 and the synod approved such ordination "in principle" over 10 years ago.)

In August came the death of Dr. Cynthia Wedel, the last of a number of great Episcopal women who pioneered in Episcopal, Anglican, and ecumenical leadership roles in the 1960s and 1970s. In September, the U.S. House of Bishops urged caution in consecrating women bishops here, strongly suggesting we wait until after Lambeth 1988 to take such a step.

All these events leave me feeling sad about the prospects for women keeping the word of God in the Christian church today, certainly in my small corner of that church. We will miss Dr. Wedel, along with Marion Kelleran, Pauli Murray, and Betsy Rodenmayer, all recently deceased, not only for the leadership they exercised and for the mentors they were for many of us, but because they don't seem to have women successors among the church's leaders. Were they the first in so many areas only to be the last as well?

Perhaps women's leadership is more diffuse now, many women doing the jobs that only a few were allowed to do a generation ago. Woman's voice is no longer univocal (indeed it never was) and no one person or small group can represent "the women" anymore. If so, well and good, but I wonder. In the Episcopal Church women have been priests for almost thirteen years, deacons for sixteen, and the backbone of most parishes for over two hundred years. Where are the women rectors of "cardinal parishes," the ordained women on the national church staff? Where are the women, lay and ordained, who chair diocesan standing committees of the General Convention House of Deputies? Where are the Episcopal women in the leadership roles in the Anglican Consultative Council and in national and international ecumenical organizations? I know there are a few, but not nearly enough.

And perhaps, symbolically, most important and telling, where are the women in the House of Bishops? It is embarrassing to be part of a church where one house of its bicameral legislature excludes women entirely. It is even more embarrassing to hear members of that house describe it as "the most exclusive men's club in America" and mean it, or to hear them chat about which members attended which men's college and belonged to what fraternity. I suppose that goes on in the U.S. Senate in spite of the presence of a few women, but it is no way to run a country or a church.

It is amusing in a bittersweet way to watch the House of Bishops debate the matter of women bishops. They acknowledge that the canons of the Episcopal Church clearly allow for women bishops as they do women deacons and priests, so we don't hear many arguments about why women can't be bishops. We do hear arguments about timing and disunity and pain and suffering on the part of male bishops who have stuck it out despite women priests but who could not tolerate women bishops. These arguments we have heard before—when laywomen threatened to invade the lay order of the House of Deputies in the 1950s and 1960s and when women clergy threatened the clergy order of the same house in the 1970s. A different ox is being gored, but the cries of its owners are similar to cries we've heard before.

It is ironic that the bishops have given the question so much time, since they are the only group in the Episcopal Church who do not normally vote for bishops. Bishops are elected in our polity by clergy (deacons and presbyters) and lay people. True, diocesan bishops do call for the election of suffragans and coadjutors, but they do not have a vote as to who will be selected by the diocesan convention. The House of Bishops may, by majority vote, refuse to consent to the election of a particular person (and have done so in the past, most often on grounds of churchmanship or alleged heresy), but this power is negative and after the fact. It is a collective veto also granted to diocesan standing committees. Members of the House of Bishops have twice indicated they would not veto a bishop-elect *because* she was a woman, but they have also asked the dioceses not to put them to the test before Lambeth 1988.

Meanwhile, God is undoubtedly calling women to be bishops. Fine candidates have emerged in a number of Episcopal elections over the last few years and, were it not for the plea to wait until after Lambeth 1988, I suspect we would already have at least one woman bishop and that several more would be elected in the next two years. But the siren cry of "wait"—most insistently keening from England but not absent among American bishops—is heard by the electors. They are decent folk and do not want to cause any pain or suffering they can avoid. (Women's pain and suffering is apparently part of our natural condition and therefore not to be considered.)

So I feel sad about women's leadership prospects as I think about Mary this Christmas. Hearing the will of God and keeping it is complicated by the church's preference for women who bear and nurture sons who turn out well.

Yet sometimes in these dark December days I wonder what would happen if we did hear the word of God and kept it. Suppose women who are called to be bishops heard the call not only from God but from their fellow Christians as well. Suppose Anglicans in New Zealand and Canada and Hong Kong and Brazil and Kenya and the United States and Uganda and all the Anglican provinces that have women priests (and even perhaps some that don't) elected and ordained a number of women bishops in the next two years and presented Lambeth 1988 with the fact rather than the theory. That would certainly change the debate just as the fact of women priests changed the debate on that issue here in the United States and made it real.

In my fantasy these women bishops would be elected and ordained within the structures of their own provincial churches. They would be regular suffragan (even—dare we hope—diocesan) bishops, canonically chosen and certified. Failing that, for the weight of caution is very strong in regular channels, some of them might have been chosen as special bishops to women in their respective churches.

In the American church we have a special suffragan bishop for the Armed Forces, whose duty is to minister to men and women in the military wherever they may be stationed. Military chaplains are responsible to their own diocesan bishops (where they are canonically resident), but they do have someone to turn to for pastoral care and advice who is especially charged with ministry to the military.

Perhaps we could use that model to create several suffragan bishops for women, whose responsibilities would be to provide pastoral care and advice to the women of the church. We know that such "extraterritorial" bishops can function in our system. We also know that women would welcome the pastoral care and advice of other women as we develop new roles and leadership styles in a very changed world. There would need to be not one but several such bishops. One thing we have learned over the years is that no woman should be asked to take on such a burden by herself.

Suppose Lambeth 1988 had to deal with real women bishops from all over the world. No longer could the idea of women bishops be considered "A hare-brained American scheme," but must be taken seriously as a vocation whose time has come. The rhetoric about pain and disunity would be minimized as it was with priesthood after the fact. To paraphrase Shakespeare, "Men have died from time to time, and worms have eaten them, but not for love—or for clergywomen."

Best of all, for my fantasy to come to pass women ourselves would have had to take leadership in the church and to have insisted that our voice be heard. We would have truly learned the great thing about Mary—not that her son turned out well or badly, but that she heard the word of God and kept it. Alleluia!

Notes: Why I Stay in the Church

Preached at Trinity Methodist Church, Chester, Pennsylvania
(September 29, 1974)

II Last 200 years has meant great changes in women's lives
   more rapid than the 20 centuries before
   A) 1) women have been educated
      2) women have gotten political + economic rights
      3) women have joined workforce as independent earners
      4) women have gained control over own bodies
   B) Yet in none of these areas (w. possible exception of female
      literacy) has church taken the lead
      1) churches opposed women's suffrage
      2) churches opposed + still oppose ERA. Also don't acknowl-
         edge working women + change in lifestyle of women
      3) churches opposed + still oppose abortion, birth control etc.
   C) Not all churches of course—but these are the voices one
      hears—same sorry progression of anti-feminine rhetoric
      which has served for centuries
         e.g., July 29th—young clergyman opposed ordaining women
         breaking peace between Adam + Eve
         sight, smell, sound of perversion
         stones into bread
      or e.g., debate on ERA
         quote Paul at length (+ out of context)
         quote Genesis story (but only one)

D) No wonder feminists have long since given up on churches—
where are young women this morning—not here, nor in my
church—they've gotten the message they're not wanted

III So why do I stay?—Why have I ministered for 10 years in a church
that doesn't want me —why did I bother with July 29th ordination?
Why are there women in all denominations who take on the insults +
degradation
   A) First, because there are so many women my sisters in churches
      who are being denied the Gospel message. bad for them + for
      Christ's church—
   B) 2ndly—because the Gospel message is more important than
      our failure to hear it
      1) St Joan's alliance "We are feminists because we are Chris-
         tians—we heard what he said to Martha + Mary
         We know who discovered the empty tomb—we know
         Christ intends women to be full people in the world
      2) We know that "faith is the assurance of things hoped for—
         conviction of things not seen"—
      3) church has future as well as past—personhood for women is
         God's will—for the church as well as the world
   C) My sisters + I want to bring that message of faith back to the
      church where it belongs + from where it came—It took cen-
      turies to get rid of slavery (w. churchs defending it on scrip-
      tural evidence) but eventually those who had faith that it was
      wrong were vindicated both in church + society

IV My parish church, Church of Advocate in N. Phila where I was
ordained priest has sign out front "This church lives the Gospel"—
anyone who knows N. Phila + that church's involvement in fighting
hunger + poverty + injustice knows that to be true—
   A) Women are trying to "live the Gospel"—
In hope + faith that kingdom will come when whole church can live
out gospel—full personhood for everyone
   B) Meanwhile I have faith in spite of the evidence
      assurance of things hoped for
      conviction of things not seen

C) + it's this faith that makes it possible for me to stay in an
   anti-woman church
   faith gives me the strength to engage in tender loving
        defiance—to make this my ministry for as long as it takes—
   I am certain God's will is being worked out + that we shall
        overcome—even + especially ourselves
            Amen.

PART FOUR

SETTING
THE CAPTIVES
FREE

Introduction to Part Four
Setting the Captives Free

In the years that followed the Philadelphia Ordination and, subse-quently, the passage of women's ordination legislation by the 1976 General Convention of the Episcopal Church, Sue Hiatt continued to weave together, as a priest, threads of her long-standing commitments to racial and economic justice-making, peace advocacy, pastoral care with a special interest in older people, and community organizing on behalf of women and, increasingly, gay men and lesbians. As teacher, preacher, counselor, and community organizer, Hiatt continued to voice a strong feminist critique of business as usual in church and soci-ety. At the same time, her understated personal style and her articula-tion of a rather conventional liberal Christian theology often took her adversaries by surprise. The impression of Sue Hiatt as a quiet, kind, and selfless woman was, throughout her career as teacher and priest, an impression rooted in deep truth, but it also veiled the radicality of her life and witness. It often either eased her working relationship with mainstream Episcopalians or disarmed those churchmen who wanted to argue with her radical feminism but didn't know quite how to do this without appearing to beat up on a sweet Christian lady. Keep this in mind as you read these pieces. Imagine hearing these messages from the lips of a soft-spoken woman in her fifties, with a sweet open face, a twinkle in her eye, and not a hint of manipulation: what she says, she means.

The seven pieces in this part of the book represent a variety of Sue Hiatt's public statements in different professional contexts between the late 1980s and the late 1990s, several years prior to her death in 2002. Included here are a couple of essays, a major address, and four sermons—two at ordinations, one at a funeral, and one in the chapel at the Episcopal Divinity School, where Hiatt served on the faculty as a professor of pastoral theology from 1975 until her retirement in 1998.

Hiatt's poignant review essay of Pauli Murray's work (written in 1988, and first published in the *Journal of Feminist Studies in Religion*) reflects not only her abiding respect for her sister priest—the first African-American woman priest in the United States—but moreover Hiatt's sense of regret that she had not known Pauli Murray better during her lifetime (Murray died in 1985) and had mistaken Murray's strategic choices, forged over a lifetime of struggle as both black and female, for a rather half-hearted endorsement of her feminist Episcopal sisters. This essay offers us a window into Sue Hiatt's sense of her own vulnerabilities in relation to other feminist Christians and the question of how she might be misunderstood by those who would fault her for her own strategic choices—for example, the choice to stay in the church, or to have gotten ordained in the first place.

As she had cautioned in 1979, in Sandra Hughes Boyd's ordination, Sue Hiatt's concern that women priests are becoming "honorary men" grows stronger over time. In her address to the faculty and trustees of Regis College, which was awarding her an honorary doctorate in 1988, Hiatt urges women "not only to enter but to transform the profession." In sermons at the ordinations of her former students Alice O'Donovan (1988) and ten years later Jean Austin (1998), Hiatt considers what a "transformed" sense of ministry will look like, focusing on the daily, often lonely, claims of service to those at the margins and on justice-making as the core of Christian ministry for everyone, regardless of their particular church or denomination. Alice O'Donovan, for example, was being ordained into the ministry of the United Church of Christ. These two sermons, like the one preached in 1979 at the ordination of Sandra Hughes Boyd, exemplify the many sermons preached by Hiatt at the ordinations of her former students over a twenty-five-year period.

In 1990, Sue Hiatt's former student and close friend Karl Laubenstein died of AIDS. It was his wish that Hiatt preach at his funeral. As an openly gay man, Laubenstein's pursuit of ordination in the Episcopal Church had scandalized the Episcopal bishop of Massachusetts in the 1980s, but thanks to his tenacity and "rocklike integrity," in Hiatt's words, Karl Laubenstein had been ordained by Bishop Coleman McGehee of Michigan, a champion of justice in its many forms. As a bilingual priest, Laubenstein had returned to the Boston area to work in a parish with a large Latino congregation. Sue Hiatt's declaration, in this funeral homily, that Karl "was and remains a priest" was both a powerful affirmation of the life of the human spirit beyond the grave and an emphatic statement of solidarity with gay men and lesbians, whose champion she had become.

We have included the Florence Nightingale homily, preached at the Episcopal Divinity School in 1990, because—like the Pauli Murray essay—it reflects Hiatt's awareness of the important lines of continuity between women of different generations and cultures, including especially those who have paved the way for younger generations of women who will follow. This sermon is, at heart, a lament for the unrecognized vocations of women like Florence Nightingale who might themselves have been priests had the church paid them any mind. To those women, past and future, Hiatt's commends a vocation of troublemaking. Always, she admonishes her sisters against making peace with any oppression, including their own.

Beginning with the war in Vietnam in the 1960s, Sue Hiatt had been an outspoken opponent of the United States' military assaults on other nations and cultures. In 1991, as the U.S. undertook the war in the Persian Gulf (its first war in Iraq), Hiatt wrote forcefully against it in *The Witness* magazine. Here she not only denounces George H.W. Bush's decision to go to war but also the church's acquiescence. She does commend Presiding Bishop Edmund Browning for his refusal to bless this war, as had been requested by President Bush, an Episcopalian, but she writes almost apologetically on behalf of most Christians who don't seem to know how to advocate nonviolence as a way of following Jesus. Sue Hiatt comes across in these few pages as both a radical pacifist and a beautifully nuanced pastoral counselor to all those Christian leaders and followers who simply don't know how to oppose war. Like any genuine prophet, Hiatt identifies with the perplexed folks who support war because it's what we all have been taught to do. "How could we have failed to notice that Jesus's teaching includes non-violence, forgiveness, and a constant striving for peace and justice?" We catch a glimpse here of the soft-spoken, disarming prophet at work. It is vintage Sue Hiatt.

C.H.

Pauli Murray (1910–1985)

May Her Song Be Heard at Last

"Pauli Murray: May Her Song Be Heard at Last."
Journal of Feminist Studies in Religion 4
(Fall 1988): 69–73

While I was working on this article on Pauli Murray during the month of January 1988, a number of stressful events occurred in my own life. I was called upon once again to defend in a public forum the right of women to hold office and authority in the church. This round we're talking about bishops but the arguments are the same ones heard by our foremothers a hundred years ago when they asked for a voice in the distribution of money they'd raised for missions—arguments which appear to have to be refuted endlessly by each new generation of women. In my personal life I was called on to travel to Minnesota to help straighten out the affairs of an elderly relative and to try to cheer her transition to a nursing home. My routine annual physical exam uncovered the threat of serious chronic illness—a reminder of my own mortality.

All these stresses came at once and I was feeling abandoned by the Goddess and sorry for myself when I suddenly realized that these were just a few of the kind of burdens Pauli Murray bore every day for almost all of her seventy-five years. She fought for women, she cared for elderly relatives and friends, she struggled with her health most of her life. In addition, she worked tirelessly for the rights of black people and struggled repeatedly with poverty and unemployment in her own life. Her autobiography, *Song in a Weary Throat*, published posthumously in 1987, chronicles a remarkable struggle to overcome adversities with intelligence and grace. The total absence of self-pity or bitterness helps me to recover some perspective on my own troubles and be on my way again—if not rejoicing at least not despairing.

Pauli Murray, daughter of Negro professionals, a teacher and a nurse, was born in Baltimore in October 1910, the fourth of six children. She was effectively orphaned at the age of three by the death of her mother and her father's inability to cope with his children. Her siblings stayed together in Baltimore with paternal relatives while Pauli was sent to live with a maternal aunt and grandparents in Durham, North Carolina. She was raised by her aunt, a struggling schoolteacher, and had to learn quickly about being an only child and being a black child in the South. It was her maternal grandparents and aunts who inspired her many years later (1956) to write *Proud Shoes*, a history of the struggles of an American family of mixed race. She was encouraged and assisted in writing that book by Stephen Vincent Benet.

The bare facts of Pauli's life read as a litany of unfair disasters. She was denied admission to the University of North Carolina as an undergraduate because of her race. Undaunted, she arranged to live with relatives in Brooklyn and scraped up enough money to attend Hunter College. After graduation and time out to work to pay back her debts she applied to Harvard Law School where she was denied admission because of her sex. She attended Howard Law School instead.

Pauli was arrested and jailed in Virginia in 1940 because she refused to move to the back of a bus. She organized lunch counter sit-in demonstrations by black students in the District of Columbia while she was at Howard Law School in the 1940s. On the basis of a letter explaining her criticism of FDR's naiveté on race issues, she became a friend and confidante of Eleanor Roosevelt and Mrs. Roosevelt's teacher on racism. As a lawyer she worked ceaselessly on civil rights cases, beginning with a black sharecropper, Odell Walker, who was convicted by an all-white jury of killing a white man and subsequently executed in Virginia in 1942. Throughout her career as a lawyer, she was dogged (and often unemployed) by the double burden of being female and black. She cared for her elderly aunts in her home for many years and saw a number of friends through painful and prolonged terminal illnesses.

In the late 1940s, she did graduate work in the law school of the University of California and worked on many civil rights cases. Some of her arguments against segregated schools, growing out of her own experience of exclusion from the University of North Carolina and subsequent work she did at Howard Law School, were used in the successful argumentation of *Brown vs. Topeka* before the Supreme Court in 1954. She also ran for City Council in New York (1949) and served briefly as assistant attorney general in California. Ill health forced her to resign that position. In the 1950s, she practiced law at the University in newly independent Ghana.

In the 1960s, she went to teach law at Brandeis University and to set up a prelaw program for undergraduates. She'd barely arrived when militant black students took over the administration building where her office was and she found herself in conflict with a younger generation of people in the cause for which she'd worked all her life.

Pauli's conflict with the students at Brandeis caused her great pain. She knew how hard one must work and how well prepared one must be to make any progress on race issues. Yet these young men, so sloppy and rhetorical in their thinking, apparently pushed the barriers lightly with one hand and over they fell. The issue on which they and Pauli disagreed most forcefully was one of nomenclature, but to them as well as to her one of identity. Pauli referred to people of color as "Negroes" (capital N) and found the use of the word "blacks" (lower case b) degrading and insulting. It had been a derogatory term in her childhood in North Carolina, on a par with "darkey." The young militants had similar feelings about "Negro" (the case of the N—upper or lower—was irrelevant to them) and no compromise could be reached. They viewed Pauli as hopelessly outdated if not an outright sellout and let her know of their contempt for her. Her vast and varied experience counted for nothing in this new phase of the struggle.

The issue however was not really a word. The militant young men were put off by Pauli's refusal to "hate whitey" which they saw as a denial of her blackness. Pauli was put off by their lack of intellectual rigor but even more by the machismo image they were seeking for themselves. The struggle of the black woman to engage in a quest for both sexual *and* racial justice was painfully played out in her life for the next twenty years. In time she came to appreciate the necessity of a "newly raised ethnic consciousness" and "began to see that much of my barely disguised hostility toward the Black Revolution was in reality my feminist resentment of the crude sexism I perceived in many of the male leaders of that movement" (*Song*, pp. 415-416). Since that "crude sexism" is also present in church circles, it was destined to dog Pauli in the last great adventure of her life—becoming and ministering as the first black woman Episcopal priest.

I first met Pauli when she was just embarking on that venture in the spring of 1970 at the organizing conference for the women's studies program in the Boston Theological Institute. She was a frail, quiet person (Pauli suffered from ill health all her life due to bouts of malnutrition and overwork when she was young and poor and underemployed). She was remarkably lacking in self-confidence, yet at the same time appeared to be opinionated and difficult to work with in a group. Several years later, as reported in her autobiography, she was accused of rudeness and of interrupting people in seminary classes and it was discovered she had a serious hearing loss which prevented her hearing people when they dropped their voices at the end of a sentence. She seemed to be put off by the militancy of some of the feminists at the conference and spent most of her time with a young Episcopal seminarian exploring deep "life" questions.

Of course, I had no way of knowing she was wrestling with her own vocation then and characteristically was finding out all she could about seminary from an eyewitness. We did collaborate on a scheme to get the question of women's ordination before the upcoming General Convention of the Episcopal Church in the fall of 1970. Working with Henry Rightor, a priest, lawyer, and seminary professor with whom I had gotten in touch, she did that.

Women's ordination to the priesthood had been defeated at two General Conventions (1970 and 1973) by the time Pauli entered seminary in the fall of 1973. I don't recall her involvement in the struggle to get women ordained, though my impression was that she wanted always to give the church the benefit of the doubt and to go slow. (She was not alone in this. Many Episcopalians, among them some of the most courageous fighters for racial justice and peace, balked inexplicably at confronting injustice *within* the church. Somehow, Mother Church was above reproach.) In February 1974, I received in the mail her personal copy of her recently published volume of poetry, *Dark Testament*, inscribed with a message of encouragement and signed

"Pauli, the seminarian." She had heard I was discouraged and was trying to cheer me up.

She came to the irregular ordination of eleven women priests in July of 1974 and overcoming her lawyer's caution, was a firm supporter of the women priests in the turbulent three years that followed. She was herself ordained priest in Washington Cathedral in January 1977, and had a lively ministry until shortly before her death in July, 1985.

Of course, I knew Pauli and something of her background before reading *Song in a Weary Throat*. The book, however, was a revelation and helped me to gain perspective on the brilliant but shy and prickly woman I had thought I knew. Without a trace of self-pity the book paints a picture of a remarkably tough and courageous fighter. The theme of her life was the pursuit of justice for all (and she meant *all*—white, black, native American, poor, female, male—all God's human creatures). She was consumed in that struggle and never in her life were the odds against her anything less than appalling.

It's probably a good thing Pauli didn't live to edit her autobiography, for her diffidence and modesty might have led her to soften it somewhat. As it stands, reading it was an occasion to look at my own experience of Pauli and realize how little I knew her and how harshly I judged her. We tend to dismiss our foremothers, at least until they're safely dead. I and many of my sisters tended to dismiss Pauli as another generation, somehow feeling they'd lacked the courage to push as hard as we have and that was why the barriers hadn't fallen long since.

In reading *Song in a Weary Throat* I see starkly how wrong that is. It is *because* they pushed so courageously that our efforts have succeeded at all. They shook the foundations so that we could topple the walls. Of course it is too late to apologize to Pauli for my failure to realize her greatness, but I can and do acknowledge a debt to her that can never be repaid.

Reading *Song in a Weary Throat* also reminded me forcefully how important it is to know and recover our own history. Fragments of a song I recall from the early '70s say it succinctly: "Freedom doesn't come like a bird on the wing. . . . You've got to work for it, fight for it, day and night for it, and every generation has to win it again." In order to win it we have to know who has tried before and how.

Pauli's last years were troubled as she came up against a younger generation in both the struggles to which she'd devoted her life, civil rights and feminism. She met the same "crude sexism" she'd observed in the Brandeis students in some black leaders of the Episcopal Church. They found her too trusting of white people, white feminists especially, and she was accused of not being black enough. Pauli was of white and native American as well as black ancestry and was thrilled to celebrate her first Eucharist in a church in North Carolina where her white, slave-owning great-great aunt had brought Pauli's grandmother and her sisters—children of the lady's brothers and a black slave—to services as little girls. In her first book, *Proud Shoes*, she traced all the branches of the family she could locate—black, white and native American and ended up with a fascinating look at an American family (this was twenty years before Alex Haley's *Roots*). But she was clearly not swept up by the necessity for adhering to a "newly raised ethnic consciousness" and the old uneasiness between her and a new generation of black men continued in her church career. She was misunderstood in the church as well as the world by blacks and feminists alike.

Pauli believed above all in justice and, despite a lifetime of disappointments and tragedies, she never stopped seeking it. She just never quit. She knew what a never-ending battle it was, but when she tried to tell a new generation about the hard work involved she was told she'd been co-opted and her methods had failed and must be abandoned.

Pauli never was co-opted but she did refuse to hate and often those two things look very much alike. She's a foremother not only to be proud of, but to learn from and emulate. Her life was one damned thing after another and she faced it all with courage and integrity. Even better, her earliest love was writing and in her three books, *Proud Shoes*, *Dark Testament*, *Song in a Weary Throat* (not to mention her scholarly legal articles) she has left us an articulate and moving chronicle of a truly remarkable woman and the brave roots from which she came.

The Rev. Suzanne R. Hiatt
Professor of Pastoral Theology
Episcopal Divinity School
Cambridge, Massachusetts

Address to the Trustees and Faculty of Regis College

Delivered at Their Baccalaureate Dinner,
Weston, Massachusetts (May 20, 1988)

Thank you, Sue Williamson, for that very moving introduction. Members of the faculty, trustees, Sr. Thérèse: Thank you all for inviting me to speak to you tonight and for the honorary degree you plan to confer on me tomorrow. I am delighted and thrilled to be part of Regis.

I began my education with the Sisters of St. Joseph nearly fifty years ago at the nursery school of the College of St. Joseph in West Hartford, Connecticut. My mother recalls witnessing what she describes as an "IQ" test in which a nun asked me a series of questions.

"Now, Suzy, what makes an apple, an orange and a banana alike?"

"God made them, Sister."

"Yes, dear, but what else?"

"They're all fruits, Sister."

"Fine. Now, how are a car and a train and a boat alike?"

"God made them, Sister."

"Right, but what else?"

"They all go and people ride in them."

We went on like that the better part of an hour, my sycophantic response, "God made them, Sister," always necessitating another question. In the end, the Sister told my mother that she should count on my going to college and possibly pursuing a doctorate. Little did she dream I would receive that doctorate almost fifty years later from Regis College.

When Sister Thérèse asked me to speak here at the baccalaureate dinner, she suggested I focus on some aspect of my discipline, but
left the nature of my "scholarly presentation" up to me. That scared
me a little as my "discipline" is pastoral theology, a catch-all field in
seminary teaching that includes everything from crisis counseling to
community organizing to canon law and American church history. I
struggled for a long time about what I might say about any or all of
those things that might be interesting or edifying for you and toyed
with several topics.

Then I re-read Sr. Thérèse's letter inviting me to be part of these
ceremonies and was struck by one sentence. "Your presence at our
Commencement will be a strong affirmation of our conviction about
the potential that women have for leadership in our society." I infer
from that that you asked me here because I have been a leader in the
current struggle of women to gain affirmation and recognition in the
churches. Being one of the first eleven women ordained to the priesthood in the Episcopal Church remains, even fourteen years later, my
chief claim to fame. It is, in a larger sense, the heart of my discipline
both as a Christian and as a professional.

My discipline is, in the broadest sense, the struggle of women to
fulfill their God-given potential. That is also your discipline as trustees and faculty of a women's college. I am sure you all spend countless hours discussing the role of a women's college in a society where
women are allegedly well-integrated into all the professions—(well,
most professions—I'm sure one in particular comes to mind where the
struggle continues).

I've just been looking into Barbara Miller Solomon's brilliant 1985
history of higher education for women in the United States, *In the
Company of Educated Women*. In reading that book I am beginning to
appreciate both the courageous successes and heartbreaking failures of
generations of educators who have worried about women. Is women's
education in single-sex schools reactionary or revolutionary? It could
be either or both and while intending to be one has often ended up
being the other. Mostly it's been neither and has stumbled along somewhere in between.

A related question I would ask first (and constantly) is what is
the state of the current women's movement? What are the next steps

and how can we break the cyclic pattern of the last hundred years, where one generation's gains for women are eroded in the next generation and revived in the third generation? Women have struggled to enter the professions for at least a hundred years. (The first American mainline protestant women ministers, Antoinette Brown Blackwell and Olympia Brown, were ordained in the mid-nineteenth century.) By and large we have gotten there. However, in our eagerness to be accepted as colleagues by our brothers we have left our women's baggage at the door. We have become, as we gained confidence and respect, "honorary men."

Until very recently, women entering the professions have been content to play by "boys' rules"—to conform to whatever professional standards we were told applied, and never to wonder whether these endeavors might benefit from an infusion of what are perceived as "women's concerns," for example, such things as sensitivity to other people's feelings and ideas, cooperation as a more productive norm than competition, concern about justice and equity for the oppressed and the marginalized. All these concerns have been characterized as "soft" issues, a proper concern for women but not to be taken into the public world of work.

When one begins to speak of "women's concerns," one is on thin ice. Women's education has been set back in the past by well-intentioned people like Catherine Beecher in the 1850s and Lyn White in the 1950s who have felt that since women's roles in society were different from men's roles and largely lived out in the private rather than the public sector, women should be educated to live those roles as skillfully and intelligently as possible. The idea (to oversimplify both Beecher and White) was to bring what had been seen as men's concerns, such as efficiency, rationality, and economy into the private world of women and have women appropriate those things in their work.

What I am suggesting is the reverse of that. It is for women to insist that the skills we've learned in the private world of women—at our mother's knee, in effect—be brought with us into the public world. I am not suggesting that men and women are basically different in kind. We are more alike in our common humanity than we are different in the divergent and often opposed expectations we've learned for our lives. The danger of women's emancipation has been just what conservative critics of the women's movement have suggested—that we will lose the gifts we bring as women when we travel from the private to the public sphere. The critics' solution is that we stay at home where we can use our womanly skills. My solution is that we bring our gifts with us in order to transform the new sphere into which we are moving.

We are moving, that seems established. Women my age (and I'm speaking tonight of middle-class, educated, mostly white, American women) do not live as our mothers lived. The young women who will graduate here tomorrow won't live as we have lived. That's fine, but there are dangers. One danger I see every day is that women have changed more than men and that as a result women are doing double duty in both the private and the public sphere. Men still do not take major responsibility for domestic life—for homes and children, food preparation and laundry, though the occasional "liberated" man does "help out" with household chores. But no matter how much he "helps," the assumption is that he is pitching in for someone else, namely the woman whose "real" job it is. We women have not insisted that men take more responsibility at home, probably because just getting them to accept our presence in the workplace has taken all the energy we can muster. In order for women to bring our gifts with us to work—the public realm—we have to respect and cherish those gifts enough not to accede to "boys' rules" and leave them behind. We must not, "now that we have become a man, put away childish things." Women have not become men and these things are not in the least childish.

One of the exciting things about entering a profession where women have not been accepted—not where they haven't been, women have of course been in ministry since long before Miriam sang her triumph song on the freedom side of the Red Sea—is that we have an opportunity not only to enter the profession of ordained ministry but to transform that profession. And we women struggle continually with how, even whether, to do that. There are women priests who insist on being addressed as "Mother"; who always dress in black clerical clothing and who keep a formal distance from their parishioners. They feel it is important that they be respected as clergy and are trying by maintaining these signs of authority to gain respect. Others of us have a less authoritarian view of priesthood and ask people to call us by our Christian names. We wear whatever seems most comfortable and appropriate for the occasion and our work. Both groups are struggling for dignity for women in ministry, but we define that dignity differently. Women cannot, many of us feel, be priests in exactly the way men have been, nor should we be. The gifts of women can transform professional ministry as they have not to date transformed law and medicine and architecture. The challenge is that we women insist the professions be changed to accommodate us, not that we change to accommodate them.

My greatest fear for women in ministry is that we will conform when we should transform. I see it in terms of what I call the *Animal Farm* scenario. You may recall that in the last scene of George Orwell's *Animal Farm*—an allegory about how revolutions fail—the barnyard animals wait outside the farmhouse while their chosen representatives, the pigs, negotiate with the farmers about the future of the farm, run collectively by the animals since the revolution. After a long wait in the muck, the animals look in the window and see the pigs and farmers playing cards. To their horror and disgust they realize they can no longer tell the pigs from the men.

Several years ago I did a series of sermonettes for a local TV station—meditations broadcast at 5 a.m. daily when the station goes on the air as a public service. (You'll be happy to hear as I was that those sermonettes are not live, but taped at a more reasonable time of day.) After the taping the director told me they were very good: indistinguishable in fact from sermonettes done by Father X, a notorious opponent of women priests. He meant to compliment me—Father X was an articulate man—but I was horrified. When you can no longer tell the women clergy from the men we, like Orwell's animals, are in danger of a failed revolution.

So those are my musings on the women's movement, women's education, and where we go from here. Women's colleges have a big job ahead of them in insisting that women value their gifts as women and not abandon them when they enter the "real" or public world.

Barbara Solomon's book has a wonderful illustration—a newspaper headline from the *Boston Post*, dated June 26, 1911. It describes the baccalaureate sermon preached that year to the graduates of Radcliffe College (my alma mater) by The Rt. Rev. William Lawrence, Episcopal Bishop of Massachusetts, in whose Brattle Street home, now converted to housing for Episcopal Divinity School faculty, I currently live. The headline reads "Radcliffe Girls Warned to Stay at Their Own Firesides: Bishop Lawrence Tells Them to Uplift Those at Home Rather Than the Downtrodden." Bishop Lawrence was a long-time trustee of Wellesley College, but his own daughters did not attend college as it was seen as just a trifle vulgar for upper-class women to mix in men's affairs.

I think of Bishop Lawrence often as I leave my own fireside to go out to uplift the downtrodden, and pass in the hallway a full-length portrait of him painted by his daughter who was allowed to paint a bit before her marriage. As I disregard his advice, I rejoice that I learned at Radcliffe, and since, that it is a good thing to be a woman and that the world of men desperately needs what we have to bring to it. I hope we will unflinchingly continue to offer our gifts, and that institutions like Regis College will encourage us to do so.

How are Regis and Mt. Holyoke and Smith alike?

God made them, Sisters, and continues to love the women they educate.

The Rev. Suzanne R. Hiatt
Professor of Pastoral Theology
Episcopal Divinity School
Cambridge, Massachusetts

Sermon Preached at the Ordination of Alice O'Donovan

Storrs Congregational Church,
Storrs, Connecticut (October 30, 1988)

when—reformation Sunday—in medius res—not beginning—just
    ordering—Halloween link of living + doing
what—calling—God calls us, not reverse—been at it a long time—
    from mother's womb
to do what—act justly, love mercy, walk humbly with our God
friends—of each other as well as God

I Whenever I preach at ordinations I am haunted by a recurring
question

What are we doing here this afternoon? What does all this mean?

A) The invitation says we're participating in the ordination of Alice
Lilly O'Donovan to the Christian ministry—

B) But I've known Alice L. O'Donovan for several years + I know
she's not new to the Christian ministry. In fact she's been involved
in Christian ministry for many years—all her life—from her mother's
womb as Jeremiah tells us—as a child in the Congregational church in
Ashfield, Mass, as a college student in a Baptist church, as a young professional with the Girl Scouts, as a young mother in the Roman Catholic Church and for a number of years in the United Church of Christ
in eastern Connecticut. I have known her as a seminary student in an

Episcopal seminary and though she never was tempted to join us, she was deeply engaged in Christian ministry at Episcopal Divinity School.

C) So we're not initiating her into the ministry today. We are certainly not welcoming her to a new career. She's a seasoned minister and already well into her first professional ministerial call as pastor of the Peru Congregational Church in Vermont.

D) Nor are we inducting her into the ministerial ranks of ordained clergy—a group that somehow serves God differently + better than do lay people. I know she does not see herself joining a club, nor I hope do the rest of us.

II What I think we are doing is acknowledging her call from God and affirming it—fitting her witness into the way we order and organize the church's life. We are responding to the witness she made to us in this place one Sunday afternoon in September when she read her ordination paper and shared with us her faith journey. Alice was honest and forthright on that occasion and we too were frank and honest in our response. We are telling her and the people she ministers with in Vermont that they have our blessing and good wishes as they pursue God's work together. By ordaining Alice today we are telling them (+ anyone else who cares to listen), that she has the certification and approval of the United Church of Christ to pursue that ministry with them.

III It is fitting that we celebrate this ministry on Reformation Sunday. This is the day we commemorate our roots in the great protestant reformation of the sixteenth and seventeenth centuries in Europe. Stirring pictures of a determined Martin Luther nailing his 95 Theses to the church door in Wittenberg come to mind as we celebrate this day (often accompanied in our heads by the magnificent tones of "A Mighty Fortress is Our God").

A) But it probably wasn't like that. It probably was more like one of our pastors putting a notice on the church door and in the local paper and sitting back to await the reaction. Reformations tend to be quiet, they involve moves and countermoves and lots of waiting for reactions as we live out in our daily lives the changes—the reforms—we are taking on.

B) It is fitting to celebrate Alice's ordination on Reformation Sunday because she represents many of the elements of a new reformation of the church through which and into which we are living now in the late twentieth century in North America. This reformation, like the other one, is challenging the Christian Church to open up its life to more and different kinds of people. The twentieth century reformation (with roots in the nineteenth century) is asking the churches to recognize the gifts and ministries of women. At the same time it is asking the churches to recognize and champion others the society and the churches have long disdained—racial and ethnic minorities, people who are homosexually rather than heterosexually oriented, people who for a variety of reasons do not conform to the church's time honored ways of doing things.

C) This reformation has its high moments—as when Episcopalians elected our first woman bishop last month in Massachusetts or as when we participate in the ordination of an openly lesbian woman who is engaged in an innovative ministry with a congregation far removed geographically from her home—but mostly like the other reformation it consists of moves and countermoves and waiting around for reactions and trying to live on a daily basis with the changes and reforms we advocate.

IV Alice is good at this kind of reformation living. She keeps in mind as she goes about her daily rounds Micah's summation of what God requires of us—

A) to act justly—always to do those things that will bring about a more equitable social order. Not just to advocate justice but to see that it is done

B) to love mercy—always to be a pastor to people in distress—to side with life in the never ending struggle between life and death forces in this world. To have compassion for all God's creatures

C) to walk humbly with God—always to try to be in touch with what God wants of us—to try to be God's friend and companion on the journey

D) But the important thing is to do these things in our daily lives—not just on state occasions, not just on Sundays. Alice is steady—one senses at once that she's in for the long haul

V We are in the midst of a reformation + we're in it together

A) We friends of Alice's—lay + ordained need to reaffirm our friendship with her and our mutual friendship with God. Jesus told his disciples at the last supper that they were his friends + that friends even die for each other when necessary.

B) As we celebrate this milestone in Alice's calling (not a beginning, not a climax, just a milestone) let us each recollect our own calling to work with friends like her to do God's will in this world. As we witness her ordination vows let us each think about the meaning of such vows in our own lives at this time of reformation. We are here with you Alice and with God's help we mean to be your fellow-travelers + friends on a long and often lonely road. Thank you for asking us to come along.

Homily Preached at the Funeral of The Reverend Karl Norvin Laubenstein

Church of St. John the Evangelist, Boston, Massachusetts
(January 10, 1990)

In the name of God, who created us, who redeemed us, and who sustains us still. Amen.

Years ago Eric Segal began his wildly popular novel *Love Story* with an arresting first line. "What can you say about a girl who died?" The answer that jumps to mind is not very much, but he proceeded to write a whole book about it. This morning I ask myself what I can say about a man who died. While I can't write a book, not today anyway, I find that in the case of Karl Laubenstein I, too, have a lot to say. The man who died was our teacher, priest, brother, son, friend, lover, person with AIDS. He was many things to many people and now he is gone.

In reflecting on the power of death, Paul asks the Romans, "Who shall separate us from the love of God?" In the late twentieth century we reply that AIDS is hell-bent to separate us—from each other, from our own best selves, from the love of our families and our friends and our communities, in short from the love of God. AIDS is a disease that isolates the people who have it, physically, mentally and spiritually. It works on people's character and personality as well as their bodies and minds. As we saw with Karl if it can't kill you one way it will try another and it will finally succeed. AIDS worked its wrath on Karl for nearly three years.

Some of you only knew Karl as a person with AIDS, but in that role he was a teacher and priest as he had always been. When I asked some of his friends what to say about him today one person told me that for him Karl was the person who most exemplified the possibilities in the slogan "living with AIDS." Karl never was ashamed. He refused to be made feel guilty about the disease or his homosexuality. He valiantly resisted all attempts to make him feel it was his fault or a moral failing that he had AIDS. Many such attempts are made repeatedly by society, by the institutions of which we are a part, even by well-meaning friends and relatives who, like Job's comforters, advise people with AIDS to confess their sin and be reconciled or even to curse God and die.

Karl would not entertain that kind of comfort. He was a man of rock-like integrity (infuriatingly so as some of his near and dear will attest). When I first heard he had AIDS and expressed my distress and sympathy he simply said, "Oh well, I am in a high risk group for it, you know."

Karl was a teacher. Like many of you I had the privilege of learning Spanish—a little Spanish anyway—from him. But he taught in everything he did, even in his living with AIDS. From that first hospitalization in the spring of 1987 he saw AIDS as a teaching opportunity. As long as he was well enough he spoke to groups on that topic. He also worked with each of us as we came to visit him. Some of my best conversations with him were in these last months at his kitchen table on Mt. Ida Road. He never lost interest in learning and teaching. He brought together many people who he thought could learn from each other, even as recently as Christmas day 1989 he was doing that. He was still interested in others, in community—how to create it and how to nurture it. He is still teaching us in this service today, every detail of which he planned, and we are still learning from Karl and will continue to for years to come.

Karl was a priest. He had a passion for justice and a deep and burning need to serve and comfort his fellows. The church had a hard time acknowledging and recognizing that, but his call to priesthood was undeniable. Even he sometimes got discouraged with the church's response to him and tried to live out his ministry as teacher and friend at Concord Academy or as a lay worker among Hispanic alcoholics in the Mission Hill area of Boston.

But the call wouldn't go away. Finally, he and the Diocese of Michigan found each other and he was ordained in 1985. He served as rector of a Hispanic parish there—a parish that thrived under his leadership. It wasn't an easy ministry—he was beaten up once by a mentally ill man, one of the Mariel boat people. Others he worked with kept slipping away into the poverty and despair engulfing their neighborhood and their city. Karl wrote to the people of Ascension parish before accepting their call to be their pastor:

> Jesus Christ is liberator, savior, revolutionary and reconciler. Although Christ died for all people, he also lived especially for some—the poor, the weak, the dispossessed, the victims of an unjust society and of the evil of the world. Christ is a fighter; he loves his enemies and he combats them. Christ neither remains neutral nor appeases. In my ministry I must try to follow his example. My own must be a ministry in which I take responsibility for my own existence and for the history of humanity—not individually but in solidarity and love.

Karl lived that ministry until the end. He was and remains a priest.

As a person with AIDS he remained all the things he'd been before—teacher, priest, brother, friend, son, and lover. You all know which of these he was to you and you come here today to honor a life well and faithfully lived.

In an honored Christian tradition Karl has now become a witness as well. He is a witness to the saving power of the Gospel—a witness to how one can maintain one's integrity and courage in the face of a ghastly and relentless affliction and how one can use even AIDS to show forth God's love for us. He is a witness to our capacity to care for one another.

His life and death are finally a witness to the truth of Paul's ringing statement which we heard earlier this morning:

> For I am sure that neither death, nor life, nor angels, nor principalities, nor things present, nor things to come, nor powers, nor height, nor depth—nor AIDS—nor anything else in all creation will be able to separate us from the love of God in Christ Jesus our Lord.

Let us thank God for the life and work of our teacher, our priest, our brother, our friend, our son, our lover, our witness Karl—he whom we love and see no more.

Amen.

Suzanne R. Hiatt

Florence Nightingale

Homily in St. John's Chapel, Episcopal Divinity School,
Cambridge, Massachusetts (October 10, 1990)

Back in the early 1970s, a group of women at Union Seminary in New York put together a slide show called "Eve'N Us" to illustrate the troubled history of women and the Christian church at the dawn of this current wave of feminism. One of the illustrations of the sad history of the church's refusal to hear its women was a plaintive quotation from Florence Nightingale:

> I would have given her [the Church of England] my head, my hand, my heart. She would not have them. She did not know what to do with them. She told me to go back and do crochet in my mother's drawing room. You may go to the Sunday school if you like, she said. But she gave me no training even for that. She gave me neither work to do for her nor education for it.

That quotation has stuck in my mind for it was a sister Anglican who made it and I know so well the frustrated sense of vocation from which it springs. Isn't it ironic that a hundred years later we honor and commemorate this remarkable woman whose knock our church failed to hear, let alone answer?

Florence Nightingale was indeed a remarkable woman. She's chiefly known to most of us through the brief portrait of her in Lytton Strachey's *Eminent Victorians*. Here she emerges as a dynamo of a person. Somewhere recently I read a comment about the Victorians having tremendous energy. She certainly personified that energy. She was a great grief to her upper-class family who wanted her to marry well when her heart's desire was to serve the neediest in society. She told her mother as a child that she wanted to be a serving maid. Her wanting to be a nurse was almost as shameful as if she'd wanted to be a prostitute (in those days nurses very often were camp followers). She did manage to get her family to send her abroad where she studied at the new experimental Lutheran deaconess community at Kaiserswerth, Germany.

When the Crimean war broke out in the early 1850s, she put her prodigious energies to work organizing halfway decent medical and nursing care for British soldiers at the front. This involved wheedling supplies, doctors and space from the none too efficient nor cooperative war office and bringing out a corps of trained dedicated young nurses. She spent much of her own money and her family's political capital to do this.

Thus the legend of the "lady with the lamp" was born. After the war she was seen as a heroine in England, even the Queen and Prince invited her to Balmoral Castle. They were charmed with the image of a gentle woman who'd brought healing, compassion, and order out of chaos.

But, as Lytton Strachey records (and he doesn't seem to have liked her very much. He felt she was a manipulative, scolding woman. He even suggested she was responsible for the death of a cabinet minister she was nagging), after the war she spent nearly fifty years as a semi-invalid badgering government and army officials to organize and improve the system of army hospitals throughout the empire. Her influence was enormous, though indirect, and despite the ill health she enjoyed she was indefatigable in her pursuit of decent health care in the army. She was truly the founder of nursing as an honorable and respected profession.

But I wonder—was her real vocation to ordained ministry? The door was slammed so she took her energy elsewhere—to a place where she probably did the world a lot more good than she would have as a country vicar in a rural English parish. Jane Addams, the founder of social work, probably would have been a minister too had that been open to her. So, I guess, would Vida Scudder, the great social reformer and teacher in our American Episcopal tradition. So even would Teresa of Avila I venture to guess. The church's rejection of powerful women has in a few instances led them to greater ministries outside the church—

and we can rejoice in these saints. But I wonder even as I say it, how many potentially great ministers did in fact do crochet instead.

Today's gospel emphasizes the service expected of a follower of Christ. It's a healthy reminder that service is not optional in our faith—not something we do after we get our theology and spirituality together, but is in fact the ministry to which we are called and on which we'll be judged.

Florence Nightingale fed the hungry, clothed the naked, nursed the sick in spite of her church's preference that she not make that kind of trouble. We are all called to make that kind of trouble, even and perhaps especially when the church tells us not to.

Alas, the church still turns away people who are truly called. Some of us know that from hard personal experiences. We must work to minimize that institutional failing and injustice, but meanwhile some of us will still find our vocations thwarted. The only faithful thing to do in that case is to answer the call, even when the church seems deaf to us. The hungry, naked, and sick are still out there in abundance. There's plenty of ministry to be done and God still insists we do it wherever and however we can.

May the God who has given us the will to do these things give us the grace and power to perform them.

Amen

Thou Shalt Not Kick Butt

The Witness 74, no. 4 (April 1991): 12–13

Listen to the words of a distinguished American, Oliver Wendell Holmes, in his old age recalling his youth and his generation's youth as soldiers in the Civil War: "We shared the incommunicable experience of War. We have felt, we still feel, the passion of life to its top. . . . In our youth, our hearts were touched with fire."

For Holmes, perhaps for men always, war was an "incommunicable experience"—"the passion of life to its top." Recently, I heard Secretary of State, James Baker, speak of the passion that war engenders for him—"the deepest passions have been stirred" even in this apparently passionless man. For generations, perhaps even still among many men, war is apparently life's pinnacle—a "high" that most women don't understand. Perhaps our "high" is something else—giving birth? Motherhood? Nurturing children? In any case, love and war have been and are closely intertwined in the human heart, at least the male human heart. What are late twentieth century Christians to make of this as we face the consequences of yet another war?

The Bible is, as always, of many minds on the subject, but certain passages are very clear. The prophet Micah speaks of the latter days— some distant eschaton when God's ways and laws will at last be in effect. Nations, confident of God's judgments solving their squabbles, will beat their swords into plowshares and their spears into pruning hooks, and no one shall learn war anymore. War will be unnecessary and nobody will act out of fear. We will all sit under our own vines and fig trees at peace with each other forever.

Clearly this is a future the prophet longs to see—war has lost its thrill for Micah. But at the same time it is a future the prophet doesn't expect to see anytime soon. Not until the nations come to the house of God and obey God's law. Not, in short, until human nature is redeemed by God.

Paul asks the Colossians to let the peace of Christ rule in their hearts—to forgive each other and above all to love each other in mutual gratitude to God. (Col. 3:12-15) Paul envisions peace among the believers, not in some future time but here and now.

In Matthew's Gospel, Jesus tells the crowds assembled to hear him preach upon the mountain that they must love their enemies. This just after he has told them not to resist those who mean them ill, but to turn the other cheek when struck and to give away their cloaks to those who would rob them of their coats. When faced with murmurs at this radical teaching, Jesus reminds his hearers that they must behave better than other people. Believers must in fact be perfect, even as God is perfect. (Matt. 5:38-48)

There is not much confusion here about what Jesus thinks of violence, and by extension, war. Human nature is no excuse for violence toward others. Even self-defense is not sufficient provocation to fight; certainly hatred of an enemy is not. The Dominical mandate, like much of the biblical witness, is clear. War is wrong—some might claim it as an occasional necessary evil, but the weight of the evidence is that it is always wrong.

Why then do we still engage in it? Why does a Christian leader of a great power see it as an acceptable tool of diplomacy and policy? When George Bush asked Presiding Bishop Edmond Browning for the Episcopal Church's blessing of his Persian Gulf War he didn't get that blessing, and Browning urged him to continue diplomatic efforts. Bush turned instead to another clergyman, Billy Graham, who blessed it willingly (there are always court prophets around if Elijah or Isaiah or Jeremiah say something you don't want to hear). But the president appears not to have been upset or alarmed by Bishop Browning's advice. He did not take it seriously since the church hasn't made its anti-war message very clear over the years.

In a way one can't blame him for not knowing that Christianity teaches that war is wrong. It hasn't taught that very often through the ages. In Bush's youth perhaps his heart, too, was touched by fire in World War II. A mere hundred years ago Holmes said that as a fighting man honed to kill other men, he "felt the passion of life to its top." That didn't, and still doesn't, raise many Christian eyebrows.

The churches, with the exception of the peace churches—the Society of Friends, the Mennonites and a few others—have been unable to absorb Jesus' message of nonviolence and non-resistance. In recent years we have tacitly told people like George Bush that war is OK—not to be preferred, but acceptable behavior.

We've done this by supporting the military establishment with a far-flung chaplaincy program that includes a bishop for the Armed Forces. By contrast, early in this century another American bishop—Paul Jones of Utah—was tried and removed as diocesan for his pacifist positions.

We've done it by failing to speak out about the creeping militarism in this country. Forty-five years ago we forced upon Japan a constitution outlawing militarism—now we resent their not having to burden their economy with large military commitments.

We've done it by arguing a "just war" theology. We find cases when war is permissible rather than condemning it across the board and making exceptions only after the fact and in the presence of contrition—the way we deal with other forms of sin.

We've done it by not objecting to bellicose language in the domestic sphere—by supporting a "war on poverty" and a "war on drugs," by tittering when leaders and generals talk about "kicking butt" instead of challenging such demeaning and violent language.

We've done it by not protesting over the past decade when war was used as an instrument of policy in Libya, Grenada and Panama and more subtly in Nicaragua and El Salvador.

Many Christians, many Episcopalians, don't believe war is wrong because we haven't preached that part of the Gospel. We've told them certain kinds of sexual behavior are wrong, we've even told them greed and stealing and murder are wrong, but we neglected to mention organized murder—war. Many good Christians, including Episcopalians George Bush and James Baker don't think war is always (or even often) wrong. As ministers of the Gospel we need to work on that.

Let us look again at what Jesus preached and lived. How could we have failed to notice, much less convey to others, that Jesus' teaching includes nonviolence, forgiveness, and a constant striving for peace and justice?

We begin to redress the balance by asking God's forgiveness for our failure to speak out. We go on from there by praying to God for the strength to stand against each and every war and to offer our compatriots less evil alternatives for national leadership in the world.

A new world order can only come from new methods. Wars never solve problems; they only breed new ones. Any student of history knows that. For the love of God and out of respect for humanity let us say what Pope Paul VI declared in his stunning address to the United Nations General Assembly, "No more war—never again war."

Sermon Preached at the Ordination
of Jean Austin to the Diaconate

St. Mark's Episcopal Church, Springfield, Vermont
(May 23, 1998)

Jeremiah 1:4-9
Psalm 23
Romans 12:1-13
Luke 22:24-27

What a joy to be in Vermont and an honor to be asked to preach at Jean's ordination.

When I was ordained a deacon some twenty-seven years ago, I drove out to the bishop's home the night before for a gathering of friends and relatives of the seven ordinands with a colleague who was well-known far and wide for his anti-racism, anti-war ministry. As we drove he asked me to explain the diaconate to him, and as I described it (much as Bishop McLeod will in a few minutes to all of us here) he was brought up short. "That's my ministry," he remarked with some surprise.

When we reached the bishop's house he told him, "Sue and I have been talking about the diaconate, and I think you should ordain her as a priest tomorrow and ordain me as a deacon, since that is the work I am doing." The bishop looked at him somewhat pityingly and said—"You know you are already a deacon. You were ordained to that order before you were ordained priest and it never went away. Of course you are doing a deacon's ministry—you are first and foremost a deacon, as am I."

As I thought about what I wanted to say today, that vignette kept coming back. I knew what I wanted to say about Jean, and will do so shortly, but I didn't know what I wanted to say about the diaconate, a much more problematic topic. I want to tell you that the question of women as deacons was for many years the "hot button issue" in the church, long before women priests or bishops became controversial. I also want to mention the problem of servanthood and leadership so dramatically illustrated in our expectations for the role of deacon. And finally I want to return to the poignant problem for all Christians illustrated in the prophet Jeremiah's response to God's call "—I can't do it—it is too much, I am too young." I remember my four-year-old nephew wailing "Willie's scared. Willie's just a baby" and feeling that way so often myself.

First—women as deacons. The first reference to a woman deacon in the Bible is in the sixteenth chapter of Romans when Paul in his closing salutations says, "I commend to you our sister Phoebe, a deacon of the church at Cenchreae." It is clear there were women deacons in the early church, but they disappeared from the western church in about the third century and from the eastern church around the twelfth century.

By our era the thought of ordained women was so foreign to the tradition that the word deacon as it pertained to Phoebe in Romans was routinely translated "minister" or "servant," not deacon. Why? The Greek is clear—the word is the same one used elsewhere in the New Testament for men in the office of deacon. But we can't call Phoebe a deacon, because Phoebe is a woman's name and we all know women can't be deacons. So we made the adjustment without much thought (a cautionary tale for Biblical scholars) and claimed the tradition against women's ordination went back to Jesus and the disciples.

It wasn't until the nineteenth century that the arguments about women deacons were renewed in our part of the church. Deaconesses did valiant but largely unsung ministerial work. American deaconesses had especially effective ministries building churches, preaching the Gospel, educating children, and pastoring both women and men in four geographic areas: in the foreign mission field, especially in China and the Philippines; in the American mission field of the far West, especially among native Americans; in the slums and barrios of the teeming swollen cities of the East, and in the hollows of Appalachia and the rural South.

They worked hard serving God over a hundred years, but it wasn't until the Lambeth Conference of 1968 declared that deaconesses could be considered ordained in the same way male deacons were that they were taken seriously as ordained ministers. In 1970, the General Convention of the American Church made provision for women to be ordained deacon (and be part of the Church Pension Fund as well) and a few women began to be ordained in the spring of 1971. The decision had come on the heels of the first failure of a General Convention to approve the ordination of women as priests and bishops (there was to be one more defeat in 1973)—the diaconate as a booby prize as it were.

But as my bishop reminded me on the eve of my own diaconal ordination, ordination to the diaconate is basic to any other ordination in our tradition. Once women could be ordained deacon their ordination as priests and bishops was inevitable and so it is proving. And so we meet today, a woman bishop and a number of women priests, to ordain a woman deacon. And all of us dependent for our ministries and their strength and effectiveness on the faithful and long-suffering women lay ministers who surround and uphold us.

Next I turn to the problem of servanthood and leadership so clearly shown in the specific ministry of deacons. In today's Gospel, Jesus tells the disciples clearly that he is "among them as one who serves." He is clear about the humble nature of this service comparing himself to the waiter rather than the diner at a lavish banquet.

Ministry as service is a very hard concept for us as it was for the disciples. In fact the ordering of deacons in the book of Acts (chapter 6) comes when the twelve declare that "it is not right that we should neglect the word of God in order to wait on tables." Service lacks the dignity of preaching and besides there is a minority group in the young church, the Hellenists or Greeks, who have been complaining that their widows are being neglected. The perfect solution was to choose seven Greeks to serve as deacons and wait on table and distribute food while the twelve preach and pray, and so they are chosen (by Greeks from among Greeks). The apostles prayed and laid hands upon them, just as the bishop will do to Jean here today.

Deacons then represent an ancient problem for us as disciples of Christ. Jesus specifically said he was among us as one who served, but his disciples quickly passed the servanthood aspect of their ministry on to others. So like the disciples, deacons are ordained but they are ordained to serve rather than to lead.

At that same ordination to the diaconate twenty-seven years ago, I invited two retired deaconesses to attend. One had served many years in China, the other in Appalachia and I wanted them there to establish some continuity for ordained women with their long and noble service.

They came gladly, but were horrified by what they saw. Ordination was for them a barrier to service and to see a woman welcomed (sort of) into the clergy was a betrayal of the principles of humble service by which they had lived. In effect ordination "blew their cover" because their ministry was so dependent on their being able to be with the people without hint of privilege and power.

And how to combine service and leadership remains a problem. How can you help the poor and needy if they suspect your motives—if your credentials seem too lofty? On the other hand, how can you bring the needs of the world to the church if you have no authority and are not a recognized leader in the church? No one will listen to your advocacy reports.

So there is the dilemma of ordained ministry—most baldly illustrated in that most basic of ordained offices—the diaconate. I offer no solutions today, only the observation that clergy and laity must hold these contradictions in creative tension as we preach the Gospel.

Finally, I want to return to an even more basic dilemma of ordained ministry and particularly the beginning ordained ministry—the diaconate. Jeremiah heard God's call, "go where I send you," and declared himself woefully unprepared: "I am only a child." A newly graduated Master of Divinity (like Jean the day before yesterday) feels equally unprepared. Indeed we all feel unprepared all the time for the awesome task of preaching the word of God.

But God answers Jeremiah's protestations by assuring him, "Do not be afraid of them, for I am with you to deliver you." This is the bottom line of all ministry but especially ordained ministry—we have God's assurance, not just here but throughout scripture—that we will not be left to do it on our own but that as God tells Jeremiah, "Now I have put *my* words in *your* mouth."

And with that kind of authority we layfolk and deacons and priests and bishops will be all right. Children we may be, but God assures us that we can be God's messengers and that should be enough to see us through all these human and institutional dilemmas.

And now for a word to Jean. You are a person of great pastoral skills which we recognize today in your initial ordination and entrance to holy orders. Your diaconal ministry is already well begun, for you delight in service among the poor and needy at Common Cathedral in Boston and will, I'm sure, continue to be drawn to ministry among that family of God's people—the homeless, the poor, the addicted, the demented, the pathetic ones.

You are also in an excellent position to bring the needs of the world to the church, for you are already a fine and thoughtful preacher. You appreciate, too, the ministry of the laity in parishes, for it is as a laywoman from this parish that you offer service to the larger church and you bring with you their support and love. I welcome you to the clergy—a troubled microcosm of "that wonderful and sacred mystery" which is the church and I thank God that you have chosen to join in a ministry of both servanthood and leadership. God speed, dear sister. Amen.

Notes: Servanthood

Sermon Preached at Church of the Advocate,
Philadelphia, Pennsylvania, St. James's Day (July 25, 1971)

A) "ministry" has come to say more about authority than service—would there be fuss about women priests + black bishops if it were a question of giving us an opportunity to serve?
We've always served—we have a few symbols of service—e.g.,
ordination vows—pope washing feet on Holy Thurs—but by +
large authority of clergy outweighs service e.g., women "having authority over men" a la Betty S.

B) Yet church hasn't ignored this passage, but often used it to
keep people in their place. Xian idea of "service" has been
used to justify + even sanctify servant castes—this passage
often quoted to remind us of importance of humility and service e.g., Wellesley motto.

C) But that's not what it says—it says he who would be great must
be a *willing* slave
1) true humility not making virtue of necessity—not settling
for what is—keeping your place.
2) true humility comes only from confidence—inner certainty
that we have something to be proud of + don't have to brag—
women + blacks need self-confidence—then they can be truly
humble
3) Christians must *choose* servanthood. different from merely
accepting it—we can afford to be servants because we don't
have to prove how great we are—

"WE WILL MEET AGAIN"

The Little Lady Who Started a Revolution

From Conversation with Sue Hiatt, Carter Heyward,
Alison Cheek, Mary Lou Suhor, John Hiatt, Mickey Keener,
Bishop Robert DeWitt at Chilton House Hospice,
Cambridge, Massachusetts (June 25, 2001)

The following reflections by Sue are from a conversation she had on June 25, 2001, with several of her closest friends and colleagues. At this point, she had outlived her grim "four month max" prognosis and seemed to have reached a plateau. The conversation, which was taped, took place at the Chilton House Hospice in Cambridge, Massachusetts, where Sue was living. Several months later, she would "graduate" from hospice and live on her own, with lots of help from her community of friends, until she reentered Chilton House in the spring of 2002 two weeks before her death.

Participating in this conversation were Bob DeWitt (bishop), Alison Cheek (priest, one of Philadelphia Eleven), Mary Lou Suhor (retired editor of *The Witness* magazine), John Hiatt (Sue's brother), Mickey Keener (priest), Sue herself, and Carter. Sue talks about what she believed to be most important about her life and work. Her words are in *italics*.

C.H.

Community Organizing

Carter: How do you hope to be remembered, Sue?

I went to Philadelphia to work for welfare rights. I learned from Terry Delmuth [Executive Director of Americans for Democratic Action]

how to do community organizing, and that became the basis for both sub-
urban mission work and also organizing for the Philadelphia ordinations.
The other person learning to do it, and do it very well, was David Gracie
[priest and "urban missioner" in Diocese of Pennsylvania while Sue
was "suburban missioner," both appointed by Bishop Bob DeWitt].
David had just come in from Detroit. I remember saying to Terry, you're
the best community organizer in Philadelphia, with the exception of David
Gracie and Jim Littrell, who are potentially as good. We all were part of
People for Human Rights, which Terry started. It was a good old-fash-
ioned Marxist, not unchristian, approach. The way we worked together
was important. David was helping our welfare rights effort, defending
and getting arrested with black women; it gave us courage to sleep on the
sidewalk in support. Roxanne Jones died in the struggle. David's devotion
to ending Jim Crow was extraordinary. When people are that invested in
the struggle, they become the struggle. So David became civil rights, and I
became women's rights.

Carter: So when you identify so intimately with an issue, you become
that issue, and you became the bishop to the women. Organizing and
building community was at the heart of your priestly ministry. Teaching was not the primary thrust.

I was a faculty member at EDS [Episcopal Divinity School] *who*
would go to bat for people having a hard time getting ordained; people in
hopeless situations. I'd try to get them into churches or ministries they'd
fit in. Every one but one I've worked for has now been ordained and I'm
still working on that.

Alison: I never would have been ordained without you.

I also want to be remembered for starting the Church Without Walls
in suburban Philadelphia, an opportunity for those of us who were not par-
ish clergy and who were too liberal to be invited to conservative parishes
to celebrate, to be able to meet with other liberal clergy and laity who were
not interested in spending all their money on buildings, but in giving their
money to worthy causes. We took a dozen people from different parishes
where they were equally unhappy and brought them together. The Church
Without Walls celebrated its twenty-fifth anniversary in 1990.

Historical Context

Mary Lou: I'd like to throw this out for consideration as a helpful visual in putting the Philadelphia ordinations in a broader context. What else was happening in the world around us? For example, 1974 was the year of Patty Hearst and the Symbionese Liberation Army!

Carter: Nixon resigned in August, less than two weeks after the ordinations, and antifeminist activist Phyllis Schlafly was coming into her power, and the Equal Rights Amendment was being defeated.

I was watching a documentary recently. The Bobby Kennedy funeral train was rolling across the country in 1968, just six years before the ordinations, and of course before that, Martin Luther King's assassination. King had written about the Vietnam War as early as 1967. The documentary showed his final speech, his assassination, then Bobby's campaign and assassination and funeral train. All these 1968 events were really repeats of 1865—the end of the war, the death of the president, the funeral train, fascinating stuff.

Bob told an anecdote here about Abraham Lincoln's comment intended as a gentle compliment to the "little lady" who wrote *Uncle Tom's Cabin*, Harriet Beecher Stowe: "I understand you are the little lady who started the war?" Nodding at Sue, the connection was not lost on us. We were gathered here around the little lady who had started a revolution in the church!

Bob also told of returning to his car after the Philadelphia ordinations. He walked several blocks, passing four or five African-American men from the neighborhood sitting on steps. One said, "Hi, Reverend." I said, "Howdy do." Another said, "Did you have something to do with that service?"

"Yes."

"Those women get ordained?"

"They sure did."

"Goo-ood!" they responded in chorus.

Sue reminisced on the security put in place for the ordination. David Gracie was in charge of security, and it included a "motley" group of folks such as Dykes on Bikes, members of the Church Without Walls, and the Philadelphia police. Furthermore, the father of Nancy Wittig, one of the ordinands, had arranged for a busload of police to be nearby in case of trouble.

Effects of Cancer

After a few minutes, Sue began to speak about the effects of her thyroid cancer on her sense of vocation:

I had begun to find some excitement in retirement after retiring from EDS. I was just getting into supply work and preaching and then I had to become concerned about losing my voice, literally and metaphorically.

You become your voice. I had become my voice. I was enjoying being a supply priest in odd little Episcopal churches every Sunday. I love to preach to ordinary Episcopalians.

Mickey: I think the conversation about you losing your voice took place everywhere across the country.

Communion of Saints

Alison: You've had very little voice in the last four months. Where has that sent you?

I've been back into my head. I thought I could write, but then I have a tremor in my hands and can barely write a check. I had one interesting sad, but then cheerful, reaction from Mollie Williams, an old friend, a priest in Chicago. I told her what was happening, and she was very upset, not so much about my voice, but about my dying. Mollie started to cry and said, "I can't live without my Sue." [We were in seminary forty years ago. We were at the Democratic National Convention in Chicago in 1968.] Then Mollie said, "But I'm not going to miss you forever, because there is the Communion of Saints! And I know I'm going to see you again!" This was the first time the Communion of Saints ever meant anything to her. That's fascinating, that a church doctrine may have meaning beyond this life.

I've thought about the Communion of Saints for years. Sometimes it's the only way to get through losing people like David Gracie, Hugh White, the idea that we will meet again.

Cassandra Mantle

Bob: What is the origin of the Cassandra mantle you've worn so well?

I think I read it in the Iliad. *I was always a pessimist and that, my God, that woman is right, but nobody would believe her. I've had the reputation since childhood. I would say a tornado is coming, and no one would believe me. And it came.*

Mary Lou: But I remember your sister telling an anecdote about your mother remonstrating with you about something when you were a little girl, and your mother said to you, "Remember, Sue, you can't change the world." And you said, "Oh, yes I can!"

Yes, that's the flip side. Be negative, but don't let that stop you! Actually, all the Hiatts seem to have Cassandra-like traits. I taught a course on "death and dying," my sister has a whole bookshelf on death, and brother John here is a doctor.

John: Yes, it's like we all wait for the ball to drop. It dropped for me some years ago with colon cancer, but that has cleared up now.

Sister Jean called me about my illness and she was distraught. She seemed so gloomy that I told her, "You sound like the pope talking about women's ordination!"

Publishing Sue's Work

The gathered group decided, with Sue, that at least two publications should be undertaken about her life and work. One should be a biography by someone who understands history—women's history and church history in particular—but not someone who actually participated with Sue at the center of this piece of history. We agreed that some young feminist historian is likely to emerge over time. Meanwhile, we thought we should proceed with a second project: examining archival materials, getting a sense of what is there, and putting them into publishable form.

"You Help Me See
That the Truth Will Go On"

Archbishop Desmond Tutu Visits Sue Hiatt
at Chilton House (May 23, 2002)
Carter Heyward

On May 23, 2002, a week before Sue's death, Archbishop Desmond Tutu visited her in the Chilton House hospice in Cambridge, Massachusetts. The archbishop was winding up a semester as a visiting scholar at the Episcopal Divinity School where Sue had been on the faculty and where I was still teaching at the time. Desmond Tutu was living in an apartment down the hall from me. He and I had developed a warm collegial and neighborly relationship and, because I knew how much he—the most esteemed prophetic Christian leader of our time—meant to Sue, I asked him if he would be willing to pay her a visit. He said yes and asked if I would take him in my car and accompany him to her bedside.

I had told Sue and the Chilton House staff that I would be bringing Archbishop Tutu to her room that afternoon. I could tell Sue was pleased and the Chilton House nurses and aides were excited at the thought of meeting this legendary and much revered figure.

During these last days of her life, Sue was no longer able to lift her head from the pillow, and she seemed often to float between waking and sleeping. In her most conscious moments, verbal communication was obviously difficult and stressful for her. When we entered her room, I told Sue that Archbishop Tutu had come to see her. She glanced across the room at him and then pointed to the top of her free-standing closet. There, in a bright purple cassock, was Sue's "Bishop

Tutu" doll, standing about a foot tall, which a friend had given her several months earlier, and which bore remarkable resemblance to the real man, whom Sue admired so much. She had told me these dolls were made by South African women and that their proceeds went to some worthy cause. When Desmond Tutu saw this doll, he chortled.

Sue then looked at him and simply said, "Sing."

"What did she say?" he seemed surprised and a bit puzzled.

"She wants you to sing to her."

"Sing? Me? I can't sing well!" he exclaimed.

"I don't think that matters—any little song will do!" I was as unprepared for this as he was.

"Will you sing with me?" he looked at me pleadingly.

"Yes," I agreed.

The archbishop then stepped close to Sue's bedside and began singing the *Gloria Patri*. Though this traditional Christian anthem was neither Sue's nor my favorite, I was glad to join Desmond Tutu in this offering of praise as a gift to Sue, so he and I sang out together in our best voices: "Glory to the Father, and to the Son, and to the Holy Ghost, as it was in the beginning, is now, and will be forever. Amen."

While we sang, Sue closed her eyes and smiled. When we finished, Desmond Tutu rested one hand on Sue's and held my hand in his other. My other hand found a place to rest on Sue.

"Will you bless me?" Sue asked the archbishop.

He nodded, said a blessing which I cannot remember, and made the sign of the cross over her.

"Will you bless me?" Desmond Tutu asked Sue.

She smiled and raised her hand slightly, making the sign of the cross in his direction. "Thank you for coming," she spoke very slowly, careful to enunciate every syllable. "You help me see that the truth will go on."

The archbishop leaned over and gently kissed "the bishop to the women" on the forehead. Then he glanced at me and nodded, as if to say, "It's time to go."

As we departed, Sue's eyes were closed and she was smiling.

I don't recall anything being said between Desmond Tutu and me on our ten-minute drive back to the seminary. I remember it as a sad, quiet trip home.

Letter to Friends, Relatives, and Companions at the End

May 7, 2001

Dear ones, friends, relatives, companions,

A long silence on this end is no indication of how much your messages, flowers, balloons, and, especially, prayers have been appreciated. I have been so blessed in the outpouring of affection from you all—almost worth dying for. I've been especially grateful to you who have written thoughtful accounts of our friendship over the years. Worth writing a book about but, alas, I won't be the one to do it.

At any rate, thank you and love to you all who've been part of this journey. We will meet again, praise God!

Sue

Tombstone Epitaph at Jubilee Cemetery, Jubilee State Park, Illinois

A possible tombstone at Jubilee:

> Suzanne Radley Hiatt
> 1936–2001
> Prophet, Priest, and Pastor
> with Job (1980–1996)
> Faithful Companion Dog

Please note the year of death on this prepared piece and the date on the preceding letter, i.e., 2001 not 2002. We have written it the way Sue prepared it. She was anticipating dying within four months of her diagnosis in February 2001.

C.H. and J.L.

REMEMBERING SUE

In Honor of an Unofficial Bishop

The Right Reverend Barbara C. Harris
The Episcopal Times Online, June 2001

July 29, the Feast of Mary and Martha of Bethany, marks the twenty-seventh ordination anniversary of the "Philadelphia Eleven"—the first women to become priests in the Episcopal Church. The historic service took place at the Church of the Advocate in the heart of Philadelphia's inner city on a steamy Monday morning, and the huge Gothic edifice, modeled after the great Chartres Cathedral, was packed to capacity.

Although the Episcopal Church did not approve the ordination of women to the priesthood or the episcopate until two years later, there were no theological impediments to the Philadelphia action. And while declared "irregular," the ordinations were by no means illegal. The ordaining bishops, Robert L. DeWitt, Edward Welles and Daniel Corrigan, were retired or resigned and Antonio Ramos, then bishop of Puerto Rico, was present as a witness.

As a participant in the planning and the service itself, I remember well, as do many, the minute details of that wonderful and exciting time, as well as the eleven special ordinands with their particular gifts and varied backgrounds. Too often the women themselves are simply referred to as the "Philadelphia Eleven" and their individual names are recorded or remembered by too few. The Rev. Merrill Bittner, the Rev. Alla Bozarth, the Rev. Alison Cheek, the Rev. Emily Hewitt, the Rev. Carter Heyward, the Rev. Suzanne Hiatt, the Rev. Emily Morefield, the Rev. Jeanette Piccard (who was already past retirement age), the Rev. Betty Bone Schiess, the Rev. Katrina Welles Swanson and the Rev. Nancy Hatch Wittig should be named and remembered as both pioneers and trailblazers.

The planning, the ordinands, the ordaining bishops, the service, the church's reaction, the subsequent actions—including censure of the three bishops and the ecclesiastical trials of two male priests who invited some of the women to celebrate the Eucharist in their parishes—and the ministry of these stalwart women are each stories in and of themselves. But there is one story many forget and one of which many more may not even be aware.

The guiding spirit and driving force of the 1974 Philadelphia ordinations was the Rev. Suzanne Radley Hiatt, who recently retired as professor of pastoral theology at Episcopal Divinity School in Cambridge. At this writing, Sue lies gravely ill on the EDS campus surrounded by colleagues, friends and students who along with professional caregivers, attest to her being a treasure to the church.

Sue, who served as suburban missioner for the Diocese of Pennsylvania, truly embodied the role of deacon. She worked alongside of members of the Philadelphia Welfare Rights Organization, bringing the church to the world, and in suburban parishes, bringing the needs of the world to the church. She was unequivocal, candid and forthright to all, never temporizing with oppression or its reality. The Church of the Advocate was her "home parish" and we were proud to have her as the first of five women from that congregation to be ordained.

Never elected or consecrated (though she should have been), Sue has served as "shepherd" and unofficial bishop to hundreds of women theological students, aspirants, postulants, candidates, deacons and priests over the years of her teaching and pastoral ministry. She also was a role model for many ordained men of the church. I well remember a service, again at the Advocate, where male clergy, in order to "complete," as it were, their own ordinations, came forward to receive the laying on of hands by Sue, others ordained with her and members of the "Washington Five," who had been ordained the following year.

In a letter to Sue, following this year's spring meeting of the House of Bishops, our Presiding Bishop Frank T. Griswold summed up the feelings of many:

I am writing on behalf of the House of Bishops to express our appreciation for your ministry which, as priest of the Diocese of Massachusetts, has included more than 25 years as a distinguished member of the faculty of the Episcopal Divinity School. We are also grateful for your pastoral and mentoring care to a new generation of women clergy in the Episcopal Church, some of whom are members of this house.

In addition to commending you for your enduring contribution to the many communities this church seeks to serve, we add our prayers as you journey through these difficult days with cancer.

May the deathless love of the risen One enfold and sustain you always.

And to that, I can only add, Amen.

"Women's Ordination: The Lens Through Which She Saw Everything"

Bishop Robert L. DeWitt's Reflections on Sue,
Saratoga Springs, New York (May 25, 2003)

These reflections about Sue Hiatt by Bishop Bob DeWitt are taken from a transcript of Sue Sasser's and my interview with Bishop DeWitt, on May 25, 2003, at his retirement community in Saratoga Springs, New York. These excerpts are included here to sharpen the reader's view of what made Sue tick. Bob DeWitt was one of Sue's closest confidants and was one of the few men whose judgment she entirely trusted.

C.H.

Sue's Remarkable Effectiveness as a Community Organizer

It's funny. I remember when Sue first came to the Diocese of Pennsylvania, where she worked for me in the late 60s and early 70s. She was working on community organizing. She worked with a fellow named Terry Delmuth and she learned a lot from him. I think that every page she studied in that book she put to use in the ordination of women, because it was a project in community organizing. She pulled together people who were utterly without any organization at the time.

She was blessed with a first-class mind, which was her best-used instrument in organizing. She not only saw what needed to be done but had a remarkable ability in doing something about it.

Curiously, I can remember when she was ordained deacon [1970] and she was looking for a job, and first thing I knew she was on my staff. I don't remember thinking much about it. It's just she was there and we were having conversations and what she was saying to me sounded like it made an awful lot of sense. I wanted her on my staff. I wanted to hold her there because I thought we needed her.

She joined my staff as the "suburban missioner," building on the "urban missioner" we already had in David Gracie. And Sue was remarkably effective in going into the difficult, somewhat impenetrable, area of suburban life in Philadelphia. All kinds of good things came out of it. The Church Without Walls was one, and her ongoing one-on-one contacts with women, and men too, contributed to an impressive legacy, including the Philadelphia ordinations. Ann Smith, Frannie Kellogg, Betty Mosley, Mary Jane and Walter Baker, Charlie Ritchie, Edna and Jack Pittenger come immediately to mind, and there were so many others.

I don't remember ever having a sense of condescension on her part towards anybody with whom she was working. I think that she was in a distinct order of her own in terms of comprehension, understanding, intelligence, and so forth which made her peculiarly effective—always gentle, never abrasive, and always very effective. There was just something compelling about the way she would state the case for something then, when she got through, the case had been stated and it was hard to see that there was any other alternative.

The Lens Through Which Sue Saw Everything: Women's Ordination

Sue had a moral purpose which explains so much about her. She was interested in a lot of things and there were a lot of things she wasn't interested in, but the one thing she was interested in was women's ordination—and this was the lens through which she tended to see everything. I don't think women's ordination would have happened if it weren't for somebody who had that kind of dedication and vision about that one thing. There was something of a John Brown in her. She was a lady on a mission, and I recognize that same singleness of focus which John Brown had. We owe so much to those who have that kind of singleness of vision.

Sue was a very, very bright person who was, additionally, on a mission. When you put the two together, it's an impressive combination. You can have a lot of intelligence and not have any mission, and you can have a mission but not have much intelligence. Sue had both.

Sue's Pessimism

I think Sue's pessimism was a reflection of her intelligence. I think it was the impatience of one who is intelligent and sees what others are not seeing. There's a first-class mind and there are penalties that go with it, I suppose.

Who Was "God" for Sue?

As the framers of the Old Testament realized, idolatry is a matter of worshiping gods who are too small. I think Sue knew this and that God was, for her, too large and ineffable and unknowable to be known fully or spoken of publicly as if we know what we are talking about. The total impact of the God she believed in was beyond human knowing. I think she believed that it is blasphemous to try to name God because we don't grasp what we mean. This is very, very hard to get at, but I think it has something to do with why Sue had little to say about God, except in sermons, and even there she spoke with humility and modesty.

For the Love of God

The Very Reverend James Kowalski Reflects on Sue's Vocation
(May 2012)

What follows are excerpts edited from a May 2012 interview with The Very Reverend James Kowalski, Dean of the Cathedral Church of St. John the Divine in New York City. Present as interviewers were Darlene O'Dell, Janine Lehane, and me. Except where noted briefly, all reflections are Jim Kowalski's, with others' questions and comments omitted.

C.H.

Community Organizer, and So Much More

If I were talking about Sue like this. she would probably start giggling and say, "This is ridiculous." Even with that funny laugh I never thought she felt uncomfortable, but that she was seeing something that you weren't seeing. She was about to tell you what she saw, and you would say to yourself, "Holy shit! How did I not see that?" Sue's insights were amazing. And yet I felt that she was discovering something with me. It was a real talent. She never said, "I've been waiting for you to catch up." She was smarter than I, but I never felt that she wanted that to be an issue for me, or that she was trying to make me over in her own image. That's humility. And that was Sue.

I would hope this book would address how Sue came to know who she was. I think over time the extraordinary role into which she was cast was revealed to her in a variety of ways. What she said to me on and off over the years was, "You know, I didn't have a lot of choices." An obvious one was for her to become a social worker. She kept hearing from classmates in seminary, "Nice to have you here." But of course no one expected her to get an MDiv [Master of Divinity degree] and become a priest because that wasn't an option. But there was something going on with her where—because of how much she loved the church and how much she loved God—she began to see that she was also supposed to be a priest. She came to realize, more and more, that the exclusion of women from the priesthood was all wrong, that everybody around her was wrong. The system was wrong, these men who kept being nice to her were wrong—even though they actually did respect her. Nobody else realized how wrong they were. But Sue began to realize it. I would want to know, if I were reading a book about her, when did she start knowing this? If you go back to those early pieces on "Woman as Domestic Animal" and "God," you'll see parts of it.

Should Sue have been a social worker? Or was that just a fork in her professional road? It ended up not mattering because she ended up using her social work skills, as she moved beyond it and said to herself, and to her sisters seeking ordination, and to the larger church, "I will be a priest."

When she was priested in Philadelphia, countless people realized that the exclusion of women from the priesthood had been a travesty! They saw that this wasn't just about one woman's vocation, or about the Philadelphia Eleven. Rather, this was about women as a whole, about all people, and about our common humanity. It's one thing to say to a woman, "I don't think you'd make a good priest," but to say women can't be priests is a whole different kind of thing. Think of what it has said over the years about women, and about men, and about God!

Church people had gotten all mixed up about the issue of women's ordination. They were upset about silly things like the "impropriety" of women's ordination or about challenging the authority of the bishops. Sue came along and turned all this resistance on its head. And I think it had much to do with her training as a social worker and community organizer. She used that training to organize the other women and everyone else who was interested in this movement.

Radically Incarnational Faith

I don't think it was just that this became a radical experiment for her or that the church became a place where she could do a project. There was something much more visceral and incarnational about it. That was the amazing thing about her strategy. My experience of her was that she took all that expertise as a community organizer and joined it to her own experience of ongoing revelation. She was so convinced that incarnation is ongoing, that incarnation was not something that God did only once with Jesus. Sue was always expecting more revelation.

Strength of Spiritual Humility

I had many conversations with her where she and I were lambasting people who felt they had God by the tail. I never saw her roar with laughter, but she had this funny kind of giggle when she just felt something was absurd. And she felt it was absurd for people to imagine they know God better than others, or know all that much about God.

She was an introvert who processed her own spirituality very much within herself. I think she kept it pretty much to herself. So when people would be flaunting their "God" in the town square, she'd say, at least to herself, "How dare you? How dare you think you have this figured out?"

So Sue thought that neither she, nor anyone, had "God" all figured out and, therefore, that all preaching and teaching including her own are actually pretentious. "How dare I?" she'd say to herself. Yet, like the prophet Isaiah, she'd also say, "Here I am. Send me." There was always a part of her that would rather have been home reading a book, and there's another part of her that thought all this God-talk, including her own, was blasphemy.

Sue could be really tough and impenetrable. When she was, she could create a firewall. You couldn't get through it. I can imagine that, when she was organizing the Philadelphia ordinations, she was a force to be reckoned with. This woman who'd just as soon have been with her cat in the woods had suddenly become someone you don't cross, because she was going to win.

Love of God—and of the Church?

Here, briefly, I've added my own voice from the interview because Jim's and my perceptions of Sue's "love of God—and of church?" are somewhat different—a difference that might be significant to the reader.

C.H.

Jim: *Sue was a brilliant strategist. But why did she put all this energy into the church?*

Carter: Bishop DeWitt believed Sue's involvement in the church was first and foremost about getting women ordained.

Jim: *I don't disagree with that but I don't think it's saying it quite right. Maybe this isn't true, but what I would bet is that this is how much she loved God and the church.*

Carter: No question it's how much she loved God, but I'm not so sure about the church.

Jim: *Well, what the church could be, I think. She saw what the church could be and she loved it so much that she said, "So this is what I'm supposed to do—help reform the church so that it can be what it should be, and the way for me to do this is to be ordained and help get other women ordained."*

Can Church Be Prophetic?

Sue used to say, "The Episcopal Church stands in the tension between the pastoral and the prophetic, and we've always been better at the pastoral." It's unfortunately so damn true. And, of course, Sue herself was pastor— *and* prophet. *Sue made a decision to go into the church and insist that the prophetic, as well as pastoral, imperatives be heeded. That was the enormity of her impact—she was both.*

She could have been a political strategist—and let me tell you, we had a lot of political conversations. She was, politically, incredibly astute. Very radical and very astute. She was radical like a savvy card player. She knew when to hold the card, when to play the card, when to fold, and this was both a matter of her strategic political wisdom and her pastoral sensibilities.

What I felt in her presence, what I kept encountering in my relationship to her and benefiting from, was someone who really knew that she was supposed to be there, doing what she was doing, and she absolutely trusted that. She was sure of herself and her vocation as priest, pastor, and prophet. I'm not saying she was unshakable. There were times when she was frustrated or angry or wanted to say, "Screw the whole thing." But the reality was she didn't give up. She kept at it, to the very end.

Unrelenting Faith and Hope

She was in some sense unrelenting, and that's what faith, I think, really is. She says to Archbishop Tutu when he comes to visit her a week before she died, "You help me see that the truth will go on." You know, here is a guy who, long before we ever got to know him as the archbishop, could have been killed. And Sue says to him, "Sing!" because she wants to know that he still carries this kind of joy with him. That's what I hear her saying to him.

Then he gets uncomfortable, and what does he say? "I can't sing." This is outrageous! Because I've heard him sing. He's always singing. I mean, he's preaching and he'll all of a sudden start singing and he's going to say, "I can't sing?" This is ridiculous that he's so uncomfortable with Sue, when Sue is just saying to him, "I want to hear that you still have joy after all is said and done, and that your joy is still in view and somehow being completed."

Going Home

Toward the end, when she was living back at her home on the lake in Southbridge, Massachusetts, I was visiting her. And I said to her, "My godfather is a Roman Catholic in Southbridge. Southbridge is a dump." "Oh," Sue said. "No. No. No. No. It's blue-collar ethnic." That means down and dirty and real life and just America at its best and not a melting pot but, you know, somehow we're all in it together. That's what blue-collar ethnic meant to Sue, which is why she chose it as her get-away home while she was teaching at Episcopal Divinity School there on Brattle Street, once known as "Tory Row," in Cambridge. Her early life in Hartford had actually been fairly high-end, like living on Brattle Street.

She used to tease me when I'd tell her I never knew Hartford until I went to Trinity College and I felt out of my league because I was a blue-collar ethnic. But here she was teasing me, saying, "No. Southbridge is not a dump. It's blue-collar ethnic." And what she was telling me is, "You've come full circle, too." She was grounded in an unpretentious, down-to-earth spirituality.

I think she saw in Bishop Bob DeWitt a similar down-to-earth spirituality that she could resonate with because, on the basis of their shared spirituality, they could find ways in the church that opened up possibilities for doing the right thing. The bishop trusted Sue. He gave her projects and jobs. She used to laugh about it and shake her head and say, "These projects were really challenging and interesting." Projects like helping rich white people find ways to relate to poor black people, ways that weren't patronizing or condescending, ways that were empowering, ways that could really help bring about social justice.

Remembering Sue

We now are at a point historically where if you interviewed a lot of women in the Episcopal Church in leadership roles, especially ordination, they would know nothing about Sue or Carter or any of the other first women priests. If you ask them when women were ordained in the Episcopal Church, they wouldn't know. They would assume that there wasn't a time when they weren't. Now, I'm exaggerating to make a point but there would be a lot of women, lay and ordained, who are ignorant of their own collective history. The truth is that some women would know but there are a shocking number who wouldn't. So that's a reason for a book like this, but I don't find that the most compelling reason. The most compelling reason is to understand how people become their true selves.

Sue was so kind to me because the way I'm describing myself is the way I was and I still am. What she always did was create an environment where you didn't have to stay blind—you see, you could become more able to see and she made it just seem like we're all working at it. So the thing I'd say about my daughter Becky, who's finishing four to five years of general surgery, as well as Emily and Matt, my other children, is that, like me, they're blind to some things. We all are. They're not blind to whether women can be doctors, but when they tell me stories about how they're trying to help patients, there's some blindness they're struggling with. Why this matters to this book is that this great woman, Sue Hiatt, was blind. As a young child, and throughout her life, there were some things she didn't see clearly. But during her life she grew spiritually and politically clearer, and she began to realize that you can learn to see, and that there are disciplined ways to learn to see later what we cannot see today.

I keep thinking about Tutu's visit with Sue. Here's this funny little man, who is a saint, there's no doubt about it, and he goes to visit this other saint. But he slips and says, "Oh, I can't sing." And then Carter says, "Yes, you can." And he does. He doesn't come to his full self because he slips back into that old traditional, sexist doxology which he asks Carter to join him in. So even Desmond Tutu slipped. This would be the way I would tell this story, by the way. Desmond Tutu slipped. And if I saw him, I'd say, "What were you thinking?" And he would go, "Oh, Jim! You're on to me! Now, you tell us a story about when you slipped." That's what he'd do. And that, I believe, is one of the reasons he and Sue respected each other—they loved stories about real people, like themselves, people who slip.

If We Care, Organize and Act!

Reflections by Sue's Niece, Margaret Kramer,
at Sue's Memorial Service (June 17, 2002)

'm Margaret Kramer, and Suzanne Hiatt was my aunt and "God,"
which is shorthand in my family for godparent.

I have always felt fortunate to have her as my very special aunt. As
a little girl, I remember her plaid skirts matched with black knee socks
and penny loafers, her VW bug, her chocolate brownies, her plethora
of cats and dogs, all forsaken by people less considerate, and her gentle, reassuring ways and little chuckle.

Sue was like another version of my mom to me. She and my mother,
Jean, would sit for hours at our kitchen table, discussing the lunacy of
Nixon, Vietnam, Watergate, sometimes doing hilarious impressions of
various political figures in their soft Hiatt voices—a discussion that
continued with each Republican politician.

Sue and my mom also shared a belief in reading—excessively—and
that the most important quality in life is to be a good person. But Aunt
Sue's greatest lesson to me was that it isn't enough to agitate: if we care
about something, we must organize and take action.

In 1974, when I was thirteen, she demonstrated her values to me
and to the rest of the world. I knew she had been ordained "in a big
way" in Philadelphia, and that the church didn't much care for this.
But I also knew that women around the world cheered—and so did
I. My own private godmother was in the annals of women's history,
and I was proud to show others her bio in my encyclopedia of notable
American women.

In her fight for equality and justice, she evolved into a real role model for countless people. With those with whom she disagreed her temper rarely flared, but instead an incredibly astute remark would quietly shoot down their arguments while she managed to be diplomatic at the same time. This is a rare gift, and one that more of us could use.

She was unafraid to be herself, and was unequivocally Sue Hiatt. I never met, and still haven't met, someone who was bent less to fashion, and proudly so. Her style was unmistakable. Was it irony or leadership that led her cats-eye glasses and knee socks to show up on some teenage girls? I smile when I see it.

Throughout our relationship, Sue would challenge, expand, and change my assumptions for the better, with kindness and greatness of heart. When I was going through challenges as a teen, my aunt always was there for me. Sometimes she and my parents were divided on what would be best for me, and I still relish the moment when she backed ME up instead of my parents.

This bonded me to my aunt even more, and we developed our own special relationship outside our family, enjoying each other as people. I know also that she developed special relationships with her nephews and appreciated each of them for their individual qualities.

Years later, she officiated at my wedding to Jeffrey Stein. But before she would marry us, she insisted that the three of us talk it over first. Sue, ever the individual, took us for a meat and potatoes dinner in a dark highway restaurant for our pre-wedding counseling. There we went through the wedding service to eliminate as much of the patriarchal language as possible while still using the traditional ceremony. She was more than happy to oblige: there would be no obeying for me or any other woman!

When the day arrived, she seemed to choke up as we took our vows, and Jeff has always joked that it was because I was getting married to him! In reality, I know she was always more sentimental than she appeared; certainly this was evident in her love and care for animals.

I started a career in social work, and she encouraged me in my goals, sending me readings that would help me think "out of the box." She came to my graduation from the University of Washington and this meant so much to me because she was one of my inspirations for choosing this path.

She later came out to visit us in Seattle several times, and the phone was always ringing off the hook when she visited. The Sue hotline was in full force, with many friends and admirers clamoring for some time with her too. I realized my aunt was truly someone special when her friends treated *me* reverently! Though her schedule was busy, she always took the time to be part of our life in Seattle, meeting our friends, sleeping on our couch, advising and supporting us through challenges.

Despite all of her achievements and her intellect, she was modest, and hankered for the simpler things in life: steak dinners, summer weekends at the lake, talking with people from all walks of life, and offering encouragement to whomever she met. When she and I had biopsies at the same time last year, we talked on the phone before either of us knew the results. She was comforting and calming to me even when she was going through the same range of emotions.

While I was fortunate to have a negative result, we know that Sue was not. It has been a tremendously difficult year for all of us, but has also brought many gifts. It is obvious how much Sue has meant to so many and her qualities are reflected in the support, caring, practical, and emotional help she received the last year and a half of her life. It is an amazing act of love to witness, and our family is most grateful to you. We are comforted by the thought that our dear Aunt Sue came to a peaceful place with her living and dying after a year of ups and downs, tears and laughter.

I was trying to figure out what I might possibly say today, and I went exploring in my local used book store. I came across a poetry book called *The Nonconformist's Memorial*. This seemed to fit the occasion perfectly, but I would add *The Beloved Nonconformist's Memorial*.

Thank you for this opportunity to share my thoughts and memories with all of you—and with Sue, who is undoubtedly listening, laughing, and humbled at this gathering in her honor.

What Will We Do Without Sue?

Reflections by The Reverend Dr. Carter Heyward
at Sue's Memorial Service, St. John's Memorial Chapel,
Episcopal Divinity School, Cambridge, Massachusetts
(June 17, 2002)

There is no question that nothing will separate us from the love of
God in Christ Jesus, but what will we do without Sue? How are we
to go forward without Sue Hiatt's wit and wisdom, her love and leadership, in the midst of world crisis such as ours today? How do we
Christians and we others cope with this "war against terrorism" being
staged by an administration in which she, like many of us, had less than
zero confidence? And what are we to make of the mess in the Roman
Catholic Church which (though greater in drama and degree than its
kindred messes in other religious communities) nonetheless has been
shaped and seasoned by the same patriarchal Christianity that Sue
spent her entire life not simply lamenting personally nor resisting professionally but building and leading a movement against?

It's a question of strategy, as Sue would say. Not whether we will
go on, because by the grace and power of God, we will go on, but a
question of how to build our movement? How to choose our battles?
How to resist injustice? How to keep on keepin' on in a church, nation,
and world that urge us to hush our mouths and take off our marchin'
shoes and retire not simply from our professional jobs but from the
struggle which, as Sue believed, is life itself. This is why, following
her retirement from EDS in 1998, she revved up to continue building
the movement. This she was doing through blessing lesbian and gay
unions in Episcopal parishes; preaching a gospel of radical economic

justice-making to affluent Episcopalians; and plodding on, steadfastly, in her work as "bishop to the women"—specifically those lay women, deacons, priests, bishops, and other ministers who struggle daily to live with integrity in the confusion of a patriarchal church that remains to this day profoundly ambivalent toward strong, woman-affirming women—women called, as Sue was, at the core of our spiritual vocations to resist patriarchal power-relations throughout the church's structures, liturgies, theologies, and pastoral relationships.

Sisters and brothers, it was more than her job, more than her profession, more even than her vocation as a priest. It was Sue Hiatt's life, the very core of her Christian identity, the basis of how she understood not simply her ordination but moreover her baptismal vows—to struggle irrepressibly and without distraction for justice for all women of all cultures, races, classes, nations, religions, ages, abilities, and sexual identities.

Like all great leaders, she was misunderstood by some and no doubt mistaken in some of her judgments. She was, for example, misunderstood by those who thought that her work was more on behalf of white middle-class women than women of other races, classes, and cultures. The fact is, Sue Hiatt was an organizer and historian by trade and training who saw white middle- and upper-class women—indeed the Episcopal Church itself—as a strategic location of social, economic, and political power that needed to be organized and put to work on behalf of social justice. Women's ordination and the church itself were not, for Sue, ends in themselves but steps along the way toward the Promised Land. This larger view of hers is what Bishop DeWitt, David Gracie, Barbara Harris, Paul Washington, Ann Smith, and other colleagues in Philadelphia saw in Sue and affirmed in her as she sought to be ordained a deacon and to work in mobilizing white suburban Episcopalians to cast their lots with the poor and with sisters and brothers of color in the city of Philadelphia and elsewhere.

She lived on the basis of a tenacious faith in the capacities of her brothers and sisters, including white affluent folks like most of us here today, to help "make justice roll down like waters and righteousness like an everflowing stream," and in our willingness to step forward and offer ourselves as laborers in God's harvest. In this way, Sue Hiatt was an heir of the same hope and enthusiasm that have historically shaped the great Christian movements for social justice and the irrepressible passion for justice among such great Anglican divines as F. D. Maurice, William Temple, John Hines, Verna Dozier, William Stringfellow, and Desmond Tutu. Among those who've gone on before, and with countless saints of God still here on this earth, our beloved sister stands tall today, a great Episcopalian, a great Christian feminist leader of the twentieth century, a great Christian pastor and prophet and priest.

And it wasn't that she always got it exactly "right," though often she did. Some of us affectionately called her "Eeyore" after the donkey who believed that "it's all the same at the bottom of the river." Sometimes it seemed as if Sue's belief in our capacities to help God create this world would fall victim to a pessimism, even at times a cynicism and anger that bordered on despair. In those gloomy moments, this wise and good-humored sister would withdraw and seek primarily her own counsel and that of her animal companions like Job and Annie and Sissy and Ginger. In such moments, she invariably would be shocked and amazed if something good happened! It took me a long time to begin to understand and fully appreciate Sue's courage: I came to realize that her pessimism was not simply the flip-side of her passion for justice. It was a visceral, embodied response to what she saw when she prayed, a vision of a world in crisis and a church too seldom up to the task. The sort of vision that drives prophets mad—as Eeyore would say, "You see, it is all the same at the bottom of the river." It was, I believe, against this grim, depressing picture that Sue struggled courageously throughout her life to build and lead a movement for justice for all, never failing to believe that, against the odds, folks like you and I could rise to the task. This, I figured, is what Bishop Bob DeWitt meant when he wrote to Sue and to all of us ordinands, and still to this day does write us: "Keep your courage." Despite her vision of a chaotic world and an often feckless church, Sue Hiatt kept her courage.

Exactly one week before her death, Archbishop Desmond Tutu who was at EDS last semester as a visiting professor, paid a visit to Sue in her room at Chilton House, a hospice residence here in Cambridge. Sue had met the archbishop several months earlier when she had been able to attend one of his lectures and, several days before his visit, she had called out for him there in Chilton House. When he arrived, Sue was still able, barely, to communicate verbally—and she spoke to him very slowly and clearly: "Meeting you has been the thrill of my life. You help me see that the truth will go on."

But how will the truth go on? How will we keep our courage? What will we do without Sue? Here is what, I believe, Sue would say and—through the power of the Spirit in which she is so fully involved—what she is saying to us right now:

***We must never retire from the struggle. We must always, as Ed Rodman reminds us, refuse to participate in our own oppression or that of others

and yet

We must never get too busy to take time out, to rest by the lake, to walk the dogs, plant the irises, eat truffles with buddies, pray quietly in the morning and in the evening, "pleasure ourselves," as Sue would cajole us.

***We have to organize! Justice doesn't just "happen." We can't do it alone, not as "heroes," not as Lone Rangers or Superwomen or Spider-men. We must do it together.

and yet

We need to learn not only to tolerate the personal loneliness which, to some degree, inheres in the prophetic life. We need to accept it gratefully and patiently and learn to live in it without regret or pity.

***We need to put action over talk, the common good over our personal fortunes however great or small, and substance over style and ethics over etiquette, which is why our sister had so little use for most politicians and prelates

and yet

We need always to be cultivating a gentleness of spirit and a sense of humor that will help us speak the truth in love, like when Sue told EDS's faculty in 1975 that they needed to hire not one, but two, women priests so that these women priests "could walk back to back together down the hall."

If we live this Spirit, which is Holy, which is God, and which is today Sue with and in God, she will never be far from us. This is how the truth will go on. It is how we will keep our courage. It is what we will do without Sue

and yet

It is what we will do with her in our midst. Because she whom we loved and lost is no longer where she was before. She is now wherever we are.

Alleluia! and let the people say, AMEN!

Reference List

Bozarth, Alla Renée, excerpt from "Passover Remembered," *Woman-priest: A Personal Odyssey*, revised edition, Luramedia 1988, distributed by Wisdom House, 43222 SE Tapp Rd., Sandy, Oregon 97055; and *Stars in Your Bones: Emerging Signposts on Our Spiritual Journeys*, Alla Bozarth, Julia Barkley, and Terri Hawthorne, North Star Press of St. Cloud 1990. All rights reserved. For permission to reprint, write to the poet at: allabearheart@yahoo.com.

Bozarth, Alla Renée, "Soulboat." Published in *This Mortal Marriage: Poems of Love, Lament and Praise*, Alla Renée Bozarth, iUniverse 2003; *Accidental Wisdom*, Alla Renée Bozarth, iUniverse 2003; and *This Is My Body: Praying for Earth, Prayers from the Heart*, Alla Renée Bozarth, iUniverse 2004. All rights reserved. For permission to reprint, write to the poet at allabearheart@yahoo.com.

Conversation with Sue at Chilton House Hospice, Cambridge, Massachusetts. June 25, 2001. Carter Heyward, Private Collection.

Harris, Barbara C. "In Honor of an Unofficial Bishop." *The Episcopal Times*, June 2001.

Heyward, Carter. May 25, 2003. "Women's Ordination: The Lens Through Which She Saw Everything." Bishop Robert L. DeWitt's Reflections on Sue, Saratoga Springs, New York.

———. 2010. "What Will We Do Without Sue?" In *Keep Your Courage: A Radical Christian Feminist Speaks*, 218–22. New York: Seabury.

———, ed. May 2012. "For the Love of God: The Very Reverend Dr. Jim Kowalski Reflects on Sue's Vocation." May 2012 interview with The Very Reverend James Kowalski, Dean of the Cathedral Church of St. John the Divine in New York City.

————, ed. 2013. "You Help Me See That the Truth Will Go On." Archbishop Desmond Tutu Visits Sue at Chilton House (May 23, 2002).

Hiatt, Suzanne R. November 25, 1953. "What I Want From a College Education." Carter Heyward, Private Collection.

————. December 16, 1953. "God." Carter Heyward, Private Collection.

————. December 1953. "The Domestic Animal." Carter Heyward, Private Collection.

————. "Notes: Reasons for Choosing the Ministry." Series III, Box 22, Folder 3, Suzanne Hiatt Papers, Archives of Women in Theological Scholarship, The Burke Library at Union Theological Seminary, Columbia University Libraries, New York.

————. February 20, 1964. "Have Fun!" Homily Preached at St. John's Chapel, Episcopal Theological School, Cambridge, Massachusetts. Series V, Box 48, Folder 3, Suzanne Hiatt Papers, Archives of Women in Theological Scholarship, The Burke Library at Union Theological Seminary, Columbia University Libraries, New York.

————. October 19, 1970. "The Week That Was: Response to the Episcopal General Convention's Refusal to Authorize the Ordination of Women Priests." *ISSUES* 1. Series V, Box 48, Folder 5, Suzanne Hiatt Papers, Archives of Women in Theological Scholarship, The Burke Library at Union Theological Seminary, Columbia University Libraries, New York.

————. July 25, 1971. "Notes: Servanthood." Sermon Preached at Church of the Advocate, Philadelphia, Pennsylvania, St. James's Day. Series V, Box 48, Folder 6, Suzanne Hiatt Papers, Archives of Women in Theological Scholarship, The Burke Library at Union Theological Seminary, Columbia University Libraries, New York.

————. November 1971. "The Female Majority: Can Sisterhood Survive?" *Focus* 1–2. Series II, Box 22, Folder 3, Suzanne Hiatt Papers, Archives of Women in Theological Scholarship, The Burke Library at Union Theological Seminary, Columbia University Libraries, New York.

————. September 22, 1974. "Fear of the Holy Spirit: Women's Ordination." Sermon Preached at Christ Church, Oberlin, Ohio, Suzanne Hiatt Papers, Archives of Women in Theological Scholarship, The Burke Library at Union Theological Seminary, Columbia University Libraries, New York.

———. September 22, 1974. "Notes: Why We Didn't Wait for Ordination." Appended to "Fear of the Holy Spirit: Women's Ordination" Sermon at Christ Church, Oberlin, Ohio, Suzanne Hiatt Papers, Archives of Women in Theological Scholarship, The Burke Library at Union Theological Seminary, Columbia University Libraries, New York.

———. September 29, 1974. "Notes: Why I Stay in the Church." Preached at Trinity Methodist Church, Chester, Pennsylvania. St. Michael and All Angels. Suzanne Hiatt Papers, Archives of Women in Theological Scholarship, The Burke Library at Union Theological Seminary, Columbia University Libraries, New York.

———. November 24, 1974. "The Life of the Spirit." Sermon Preached at Harkness Chapel, Connecticut College, New London, Connecticut. Series V, Box 48, Folder 7, Suzanne Hiatt Papers, Archives of Women in Theological Scholarship, The Burke Library at Union Theological Seminary, Columbia University Libraries, New York.

———. March 20, 1975. "Jonathan Daniels: Militant Saint." Sermon Preached at Eucharist Commemorating Jonathan Daniels, St. John's Chapel, Episcopal Divinity School, Cambridge, Massachusetts. Series V, Box 48, Folder 4, Suzanne Hiatt Papers, Archives of Women in Theological Scholarship, The Burke Library at Union Theological Seminary, Columbia University Libraries, New York.

———. 1975. "Why I Believe I Am Called to the Priesthood." In *The Ordination of Women Pro and Con*, edited by Michael P. Hamilton and Nancy S. Montgomery, 30–42. New York: Morehouse Barlow Co.

———. 1977. "The Challenge of the Churches: Why Bother?" Address to Radcliffe College. Series III, Box 22, Folder 6, Suzanne Hiatt Papers, Archives of Women in Theological Scholarship, The Burke Library at Union Theological Seminary, Columbia University Libraries, New York.

———. April 21, 1979. Sermon Preached at the Ordination of Sandra Hughes Boyd to the Priesthood, Christ Church, Cambridge, Massachusetts. Suzanne Hiatt Papers, Archives of Women in Theological Scholarship, The Burke Library at Union Theological Seminary, Columbia University Libraries, New York.

———. Fall 1983. "How We Brought the Good News from Graymoor to Minneapolis: An Episcopal Paradigm." *Journal of Ecumenical Studies* 20 (4): 576–84.

———. June 1984. "Women in the Episcopal Diaconate and Priesthood: An Unrecognized Shared History." Paper Presented at the Sixth Berkshire Conference on the History of Women, Smith College, Northampton, Massachusetts. Series II, Box 22, Folder 5, Suzanne Hiatt Papers, Archives of Women in Theological Scholarship, The Burke Library at Union Theological Seminary, Columbia University Libraries, New York.

———. September 1985. "Fair Harvard's Daughters." *Radcliffe Quarterly* 71 (3): 41–42.

———. December 1986. "The Great Thing About Mary." *The Witness* 69 (12): 6–8.

———. May 20, 1988. Address to Trustees and Faculty of Regis College, Delivered at Their Baccalaureate Dinner, Weston, Massachusetts. Series V, Box 47, Folder 5, Suzanne Hiatt Papers, Archives of Women in Theological Scholarship, The Burke Library at Union Theological Seminary, Columbia University Libraries, New York.

———. Fall 1988. "Pauli Murray: May Her Song Be Heard at Last." *Journal of Feminist Studies in Religion* (4): 69–73.

———. October 30, 1988. Sermon Preached at the Ordination of Alice O'Donovan, Storrs Congregational Church, Storrs, Connecticut. Series V, Box 48, Folder 8, Suzanne Hiatt Papers, Archives of Women in Theological Scholarship, The Burke Library at Union Theological Seminary, Columbia University Libraries, New York.

———. January 10, 1990. Homily Preached at the Funeral of The Reverend Karl Norvin Laubenstein, Church of St. John the Evangelist, Boston, Massachusetts. Series V, Box 48, Folder 8, Suzanne Hiatt Papers, Archives of Women in Theological Scholarship, The Burke Library at Union Theological Seminary, Columbia University Libraries, New York.

———. October 10, 1990. "Florence Nightingale." Homily in St. John's Chapel, Episcopal Divinity School, Cambridge, Massachusetts. Series II, Box 22, Folder 3, Suzanne Hiatt Papers, Archives of Women in Theological Scholarship, The Burke Library at Union Theological Seminary, Columbia University Libraries, New York.

———. April 1991. "Thou Shalt Not Kick Butt." *The Witness* 74 (4): 12–13.

———. May 23, 1998. Sermon at Ordination of Jean Austin to the Diaconate, St. Mark's Episcopal Church, Springfield, Vermont. Series V, Box 48, Folder 9, Suzanne Hiatt Papers, Archives of Women in Theological Scholarship, The Burke Library at Union Theological Seminary, Columbia University Libraries, New York.

———. May 7, 2001. Letter to Friends, Relatives, and Companions at the End. Carter Heyward, Private Collection.

———. May 7, 2001. Tombstone Epitaph at Jubilee Cemetery, Jubilee State Park, Illinois. Carter Heyward, Private Collection.

Kramer, M. June 17, 2002. "If We Care, Organize and Act!" Reflections by Sue's niece, Margaret Kramer, at Sue's Memorial Service, St. John's Memorial Chapel, Episcopal Divinity School, Cambridge, Massachusetts. Carter Heyward, Private Collection.